Teaching Students With Classic Autism Functional Social Skills in Natural Settings:

A Program Based on Individualized Comprehensive Assessment and Evidence-Based Practices

Susan J. Sheridan, EdD, and Deborah E. Bahme, MEd

©2013 AAPC Publishing
P.O. Box 23173
Shawnee Mission, Kansas 66283-0173
www.aapcpublishing.net

Publisher's Cataloging-in-Publication

Sheridan, Susan J.

Teaching students with classic autism functional social skills in natural settings : a program based on individualized comprehensive assessment and evidence-based practices / Susan J. Sheridan and Deborah E. Bahme. -- Shawnee Mission, Kan. : AAPC Publishing, c2013.

p. ; cm.

ISBN: 978-1-937473-88-4
LCCN: 2013945508
Includes bibliographical references.
Summary: A program developed specifically for students with classic features of autism, who tend to learn best by participating in activities they find interesting, engaging, and part of their daily lives. As a result, the social skills are embedded in motivating lessons in real-life social situations, involving such things as learning to do something nice for others, working on a class room project, or waiting in a cafeteria line.--Publisher.

1. Autistic children--Life skills guides--Study and teaching. 2. Autistic children--Behavior modification--Study and teaching. 3. Social skills in children--Study and teaching. 4. Social interaction in children--Study and teaching. 5. Social participation--Study and teaching. 6. Social learning--Study and teaching. 7. Interpersonal relations in children--Study and teaching. 8. Communicative disorders in children--Study and teaching. I. Bahme, Deborah E. II. Title.

HM691 .S54 2013
371.94--dc23   1308

This book is designed in Frutiger.

Interior photographs ©Thinkstockphotos.com; cover art ©istockphoto.com

Printed in the United States of America.

DEDICATION

To all of you who have touched our lives so profoundly, we say thank you.

To our families, whose understanding and support have made this project possible, especially Tim and Nathaniel, Jane, Lisl, and Scotty.

To the children who have taught us valuable lessons and motivated us.

To the teachers who have been our models and continual sources of new ideas.

To the parents who have allowed us to be with your children over the past 18 years. Your support and wisdom are sources of great inspiration.

TABLE OF CONTENTS

OUR STORY

This social skills program was taught to us by the children we have worked with over the past 18 years. Time and time again, we found that when we truly observed and listened to the children, they showed us what they needed to be successful. They were and continue to be our best teachers.

Many years ago, Sue began testing students on the autism spectrum whose performance did not measure accurately on standardized tests. Although there were many things these students could do, they did not "stack the blocks" when asked, did not respond when asked for their name, and frequently did not even come to the table when called. After testing the students, Sue often recommended that the parents take their son or daughter to the neighborhood park and encourage the child to play with other children in a natural environment. Parents responded, "That's easy for you to say because you're not the mom. If I take him to the park, he'll run to me for help and I can't stand to see other kids make fun of him or misunderstand him. It's not a typical day at the park."

Lesson Learned: Parents need help in providing social skills instruction for their child.

After hearing this response repeatedly, Sue decided to start a summer group for young children who would meet at a neighborhood park to play. This is when Deborah joined Sue, and together we encouraged social interactions among all the children.

Lesson Learned: Having a like-minded partner makes it so much easier than trying to encourage these social skills alone.

We began with an integrated group consisting of children on the autism spectrum and typical peers. Due to the variances in students with classic autism, our group was made up of students who differed in cognitive, communication, social, and behavioral skills. We got off to a good start, but soon the typical peers had birthday parties, soccer games, play dates, and other activities that they wanted to go to on Saturdays when the group was meeting at the park. Also, the way we handled "normal" kid behaviors with the typical peers was different from the way we handled problematic behaviors with the children on the spectrum. For example, one day some of the typical peers began walking across the picnic tables. This is not a terrible behavior at a park, and we could just say to them, "Hey, get off. We want to eat at that table." However, if one of the children on the spectrum had done it, we might take him aside and say, "We never walk on a table, anywhere. That is a rule." This difference was necessary due to the difficulty children on the spectrum have in understanding that certain behaviors might be okay in one environment but never okay in another.

Lesson Learned: *The children on the spectrum required direct instruction tailored to their specific needs while the typical peers often required only minor redirection.*

As we observed our group, we realized that although the typical peers were willing to interact with the children on the spectrum, their interactions were not the same as when they played with each other. They often acted more like a teacher, a parent, or a caregiver than a friend. Part of this might have been because the children on the spectrum were difficult to play with. They didn't play in the ways the peers played. Some of them wanted to sift sand rather than building sand castles. Some refused to get off the swings when others wanted a turn. None of the children on the spectrum wanted to play the pretend games the peers played.

Lesson Learned: *When we questioned what the typical peers were gaining from this experience, we realized that the children on the spectrum were not picking up social skills by just being in the park or being in a group with typical peers.*

As the typical kids began going to their own Saturday morning activities more often, we continued to have a social group, but the only kids coming were those on the autism spectrum. We also moved the group to Sue's playroom rather than always meeting at the park. This was done so that we could have an environment in which we could talk about, teach social skills, and prime the group for the community activity we would experience that day. Since that time, we have found many benefits to starting each session in a home environment, in addition to the benefits we have enjoyed while going into the community each week.

One of the routines we have set up in each group is to start every session with a "meeting." We call this a meeting to differentiate it from circle time and other types of standard school activities. These meetings provide security in that the participants know and anticipate that a routine will be followed. Our meetings follow a format of each child telling one good thing that has happened during the week and saying something nice about someone in the room. This gives the children an opportunity to practice giving and receiving compliments and helps them practice verbal and nonverbal communication skills. It is also in meetings that the community location we are going to visit that day is decided or announced.

Through the years, we have had many children in our groups who are motivated by food. One of our nonverbal friends does not readily come to the meeting because he doesn't like to sit down, listen, or wait his turn. To address this, we created a procedure to have cookies, which he made, at the meetings. The rule was, "No cookie unless you are at the meeting when they are being served." This got the child to the meeting in a positive and motivating way, and he often decided to stay and participate to the best of his abilities.

Lesson Learned: *Everything we do has to be fun and motivating in order for the children on the spectrum to both try and do things that are difficult for them.*

One Saturday morning, we decided to videotape the weekly meeting because we wanted to share what we do in our group with others. We let the children know they would be teaching adults about what we do. One child said, "I know the rules for play group!" Unsure of what rules he was talking about, we were interested in hearing what he had to say. He began by telling us that one of the rules was not to argue about where we were going to go after the meeting was over. He was very explicit and even role-played that we don't whine, cry, or say, "I don't want to go there." Soon after that, Deborah announced that we were going to the fire department museum. That very same child was the first to say, "I don't like museums!" Others quickly joined in, also expressing their displeasure over going to a museum. One of our nonverbal participants indicated that he was not going by refusing to leave the meeting room.

> *Lesson Learned:* *Memorizing rules does not necessarily translate into desired behavior. Teaching skills when and where the children need to use them makes lessons more successful.*

We respect the children in the group and accept them even when their behaviors are challenging. They can trust that we are always sensitive to their needs and treat them well. They know this will never change. However, being sensitive to their needs may mean different things on different days. We always ask that the children do their best, but if they are having a difficult day we give them more time to respond or change the demands being placed on them.

> *Lesson Learned:* *We can be consistent without being rigid.*

As the children matured, we added more and more challenges to our usual procedures. One of these challenges involved giving a compliment to another child at the meeting. The first time we tried this, one child said, "I don't have anything nice to say about anybody." Another child said, "You're wearing a blue shirt." Several others just looked at us with blank stares. The next week we took turns modeling how to give a compliment. We continued giving and receiving compliments each time we met. Eventually, the children became more comfortable with this and even enjoyed receiving compliments and encouraged others to compliment them. We cannot stop doing something because it doesn't work the first time. As we get better at doing something difficult, it becomes easier and more fun.

> *Lesson Learned:* *The children have shown us on many occasions the benefits of time, repetition, and gradual change. Things that are challenging at first can become some of our greatest successes when we don't give up.*

One of the children began to complain about eating at the same table as another boy in the group. It wasn't that he didn't want to sit with the other boy; it was because the other boy chewed with his mouth open and didn't wipe his face, which was grossing him out. Our first inclination was to insist that we all eat together because we are friends. However, we realized that what we really needed to do was to teach the boy to chew with his mouth closed and use a napkin. This solved the problem!

> **Lesson Learned:** *We can't ask others to ignore behaviors that are unpleasant or rude. Sometimes we need to just teach basic manners.*

> **Final Lesson Learned:** *After experiencing success in a safe and accepting environment, the children from our groups were often more willing to participate in other, more challenging, environments.*

These are stories of how and what we learned from our friends on the autism spectrum. It has been interesting to see young people emerge as leaders who in other environments would not be leaders. It is equally as interesting to see young people who don't do what the adults suggest but do what peers or those of similar age request.

In the following pages you will learn about the social skills program that has been developed and implemented thanks to the many lessons we've learned from our friends on the autism spectrum. We encourage you to use this program to experience the same joy that we have as you watch children on the autism spectrum grow and develop social skills that help to make their lives happier and more meaningful.

OVERVIEW OF THE PROGRAM

This program was developed specifically for students with classic features of autism. These students tend to learn best by participating in activities they find interesting, engaging, and part of their daily lives. Such experiences provide the context in which students learn and apply social skills that are necessary to interact successfully with others in the settings and situations where they will be used.

We feel strongly that, especially when working with individuals with classic features of autism, it is important to acknowledge not only the skills that need to be developed but also the present behaviors that may be preventing social interactions from occurring. Many students may want to have friends but are not at a point where they can demonstrate behaviors that allow or encourage social interactions. For example, some students with autism may grab others' food, chew with their mouth open, do not use a napkin, deliberately spill drinks, or exhibit other behaviors that make it difficult for anyone to watch them eat or eat next to them.

It is not possible for students with autism to share or play with others if peers don't want to be around them due to challenging eating habits, frequent meltdowns, or non-compliant behaviors. Consequently, this program includes assessment and teaching of such foundational skills as manners, environmental regulation, the willingness to do non-preferred things, and transition skills. The social skills taught in this program are embedded in motivating lessons and are not presented as stand-alone skills outside of a real-life social context. The students for whom the program was developed do not easily generalize social skills. Sometimes they use a learned social skill inappropriately, such as trying to shake hands with a friend in the hallway at school – something typical peers would never do. In order to avoid inappropriate social behaviors, these skills are taught in real social situations involving such things as learning to do something nice for others, working on a classroom project or waiting in a cafeteria line.

The program provides the foundational skills necessary for learning more sophisticated social interaction skills. This does not preclude higher-functioning students from participating – gaining valuable insights and skills, or reinforcing their social skills while serving as models for those with greater needs.

Learning social skills is often perplexing, challenging, and not very motivating for students on the autism spectrum. Therefore, the lessons are developed to give students the opportunity to learn and practice social skills through activities they enjoy.

Components of the Program

Functional Social Skills Assessment (FSSA)

- Consists of 13 functional social skill areas
- Follows a progressive sequence of skills, when appropriate
- Assesses skills appropriate for school, home, and community
- Incorporates areas of special needs for individuals with classic autism
- Differentiates four skill levels – acquisition, fluency, maintenance, and generalization
- Contains a chart of the assessment categories addressed in each lesson
- Includes instruction for using the assessment

Visual Social Skills Profile (VSSP)

- Highlights students' social skills development on a series of circular charts
- Corresponds with the Functional Social Skills Assessment

IEP Goals and Objectives

- Suggest how to write IEP goals and objectives that align with the results of the assessment
- Provide examples of observable and measurable goals and objectives

Evidence-Based Practices

- Describe the evidence-based practices used in this program
- Include a chart of the strategies that are incorporated into each lesson

Lessons

- Consist of 10 detailed lessons for teaching the targeted social skills over a period of time determined by the needs and abilities of the students
- Guide the teaching of social skills in context within an array of activities
- Incorporate social skills from a variety of categories
- Meet the needs of students with differing levels of social skills
- Focus on the application of taught social skills
- Follow a consistent format for ease of use. Each lesson includes the purpose of the lesson, targeted skill categories from the Functional Social Skills Assessment, recommended evidence-based practices, considerations for the lesson, materials needed, steps in implementing the lesson, extension activities (for parents and for students who are higher functioning), and references and resources. Some lessons may include adaptations, examples, or specific sections that apply only to that lesson.

Program Steps

The following chart illustrates the various components of the program and the order in which they are completed.

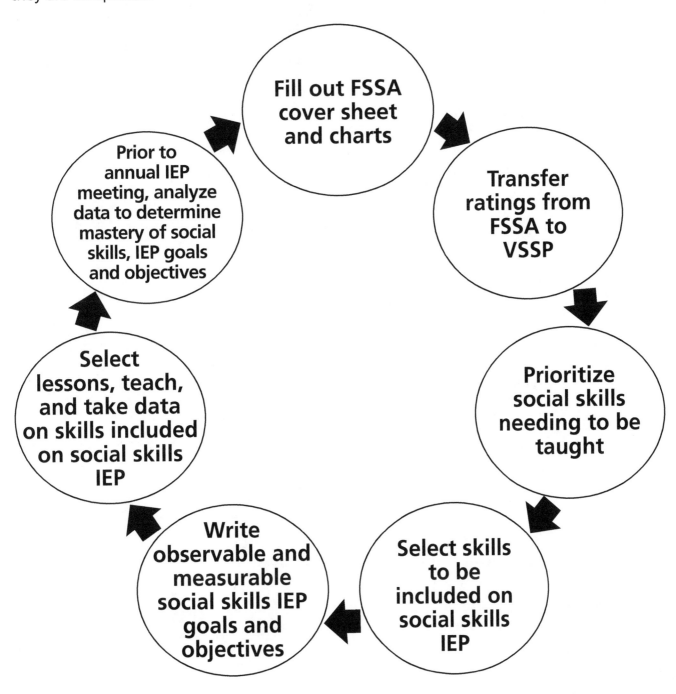

GETTING READY TO TEACH

I n order to have a successful teaching/learning experience of any kind, the teacher, instructor, or parent must understand what the student knows, understands, and is able to do. Without such a foundation, it is easy to overestimate what the student with classic autism really understands or, on the other hand, to set expectations that are too low.

The Functional Social Skills Assessment (FSSA)

All teaching begins with assessment. With this in mind, the Functional Social Skills Assessment (FSSA) was developed to assess not only the student's social behaviors but also the student's levels of learning. It is especially important to know if a student is just acquiring a skill, if the skill is established but needs practice, or, if the student uses the skill independently, where, when, and with whom it is needed. The FSSA also encourages raters to take into consideration contextual changes that need to be addressed. For example, some social skills are different when used with peers than with adults. Other skills may change depending on the environment, such as whether the student is at home, in a classroom, or in the community. The FSSA is sensitive to these considerations in the section entitled Ability to Communicate Effectively With Communication Partner by separating the rating of how the identified skills are used with peers from how they are used with adults. It is suggested that raters use the Comments column to explain if there are differences in skill levels based on the environment, mood, people with whom the student is interacting, or other considerations.

The Common Core State Standards (http://www.corestandards.org) provide teachers and parents with a set of knowledge and skills that prepare students for their entry into a global, competitive society. Parents and teachers share the same goals – to help children be prepared for life, relationships, school, and work experiences they will have as adults. The skills included in the FSSA are foundational in the development of individuals on the autism spectrum to become as independent as possible and prepared for life after high school. As such, many of the skills that constitute the FSSA are prerequisites of those in the Common Core State Standards. In the world of standardized testing that exists in school districts in every state across the country today, students with even the most severe disabilities are expected to successfully participate in state assessments or alternative assessments. A student's competence in the important social skills found in the FSSA will impact their performance during these assessments, as well as help them reach their potential in all areas of adult life.

Upon completing the FSSA for an individual student, it may be daunting to see the number of skills that need to be developed. It is important, therefore, to prioritize the skills based on each student's individual needs, age, abilities, present environment, parent priorities, and future plans. This prioritized list is then used to develop observable and measurable social skills IEP goals and objectives for the student.

Challenges in social skills are a defining characteristic of autism spectrum disorders. The FSSA may also be used to show progress, which is often difficult to measure. It is essential that social skills are taught and progress measured so that as improvements in socialization are made, new expectations and challenges can be presented and taught. The FSSA was designed to be used once a year over a number of years to show how a student has grown when the progress is often so subtle it might be overlooked.

The FSSA was also developed so that the adult working with a student might see the potential range of social skills within each of the 13 designated areas. Perhaps the teacher, instructor, or parent sees a skill on the chart that should be taught to a specific student in a different environment. The student is then taught that skill in each setting where it is needed.

Our hope is that the FSSA will be used in whatever way benefits the student, instructor, family, and community in which the individual lives and functions.

THE FUNCTIONAL SOCIAL SKILLS ASSESSMENT (FSSA)

Please check the boxes indicating the student's current level of learning for each skill using the following criteria:

0 = this skill has never been observed; requires many prompts, reinforcers, and time to demonstrate (acquisition)
1 = this is an emerging skill, requires fewer prompts; reinforced when skill is demonstrated within designated time (fluency)
2 = this skill is performed independently, without prompts or reinforcers (maintenance)
3 = this skill is performed independently in various environments, with different people, materials and directions (generalization)

Mark the items by placing a check ($\checkmark$) in the appropriate column 0 – 1 – 2 – 3 to indicate the student's level of learning on that skill at this time. Please complete the following information each time the FSSA is updated in the color of ink/pencil used in marking each item on the chart.

Please fill out the Visual Social Skills Profile (VSSP) by transferring the information obtained on the checklist to the circular charts (pages 29-33) using the directions given for the VSSP.

Name of Student:_____ Date of Birth: _____ Age: _____

Assessment Date: _____ Name of Assessor: _____ Relationship to Student: _____
Method of Assessment (check one or more):
___ observation in natural situations ___ gave student task/observed ___ previous knowledge of student
___ information from informant (relationship to student: _____) ___ other: _____
Mode of Student Communication: ___ verbal ___ pointing/gestures ___ pictures ___ voice output device

Assessment Date: _____ Name of Assessor: _____ Relationship to Student: _____
Method of Assessment (check one or more):
___ observation in natural situations ___ gave student task/observed ___ previous knowledge of student
___ information from informant (relationship to student: _____) ___ other: _____
Mode of Student Communication: ___ verbal ___ pointing/gestures ___ pictures ___ voice output device

Assessment Date: _____ Name of Assessor: _____ Relationship to Student: _____
Method of Assessment (check one or more):
___ observation in natural situations ___ gave student task/observed ___ previous knowledge of student
___ information from informant (relationship to student: _____) ___ other: _____
Mode of Student Communication: ___ verbal ___ pointing/gestures ___ pictures ___ voice output device

ABILITY TO COMMUNICATE EFFECTIVELY WITH COMMUNICATION PARTNER		0	1	2	3	
There is often a significant difference in the way a student communicates with adults versus peers; therefore, rate the student's communication skills with adults and with peers. *All responses should reflect the student's social skills demonstrated in a manner commensurate with his/her communication abilities.*		Acquisition	Fluency	Maintenance	Generalization	**COMMENTS**
1 Responds when called by name	(WITH ADULT PARTNER)					
	(WITH PEER PARTNER)					
2 Responds to greetings and farewells	(ADULT)					
	(PEER)					
3 Says (initiates) goodbye	(ADULT)					
	(PEER)					
4 Obtains other's attention in a socially acceptable manner	(ADULT)					
	(PEER)					
5 Faces communication partner when communicating	(ADULT)					
	(PEER)					
6 Establishes eye contact when initiating communication	(ADULT)					
	(PEER)					
7 Matches tone of voice to affect of communication	(ADULT)					
	(PEER)					

FSSA continued.

ABILITY TO COMMUNICATE EFFECTIVELY WITH COMMUNICATION PARTNER		0 Acquisition	1 Fluency	2 Maintenance	3 Generalization	COMMENTS
8	Matches facial expression to affect of communication	(ADULT)				
		(PEER)				
9	Responds when given a choice	(ADULT)				
		(PEER)				
10	Requests desired item when asked, "What do you want?"	(ADULT)				
		(PEER)				
11	Initiates requests for desired items	(ADULT)				
		(PEER)				
12	Greets others	(ADULT)				
		(PEER)				
13	Initiates requests for assistance or a break	(ADULT)				
		(PEER)				
14	Follows directions	(ADULT)				
		(PEER)				

FSSA continued.

15	Uses social conventions (please, thank you, excuse me, etc.)	(ADULT)					
		(PEER)					
16	Initiates a social interaction	(ADULT)					
		(PEER)					
17	Requests to join an activity	(ADULT)					
		(PEER)					
18	Shares information or experiences when asked	(ADULT)					
		(PEER)					
19	Selects words appropriate to communication partner	(ADULT)					
		(PEER)					
20	Asks to use other people's belongings	(ADULT)					
		(PEER)					
21	Waits for communication partner to finish speaking before walking away	(ADULT)					
		(PEER)					
22	Asks questions or comments on statements made by communication partner	(ADULT)					
		(PEER)					

FSSA continued.

	ABILITY TO COMMUNICATE EFFECTIVELY WITH COMMUNICATION PARTNER		0 Acquisition	1 Fluency	2 Maintenance	3 Generalization	COMMENTS
23	Joins a conversation by commenting on or asking about an item belonging to another person	(ADULT)					
		(PEER)					
24	Engages in conversation topics selected by others	(ADULT)					
		(PEER)					
25	Waits for communication partner to finish speaking before responding	(ADULT)					
		(PEER)					
26	Disengages from communication upon hearing social convention for ending conversation ("Thank you for telling me that," "It's been nice talking to you.")	(ADULT)					
		(PEER)					
27	Uses a social convention to disengage from a conversation at a socially acceptable time (waves goodbye; smiles; says, "See ya.")	(ADULT)					
		(PEER)					
28	Matches voice level to proximity of communication partner	(ADULT)					
		(PEER)					
29	Uses relationship to communication partner to determine physical proximity	(ADULT)					
		(PEER)					

FSSA continued.

	ABILITY TO COMMUNICATE EFFECTIVELY WITH COMMUNICATION PARTNER		0 Acquisition	1 Fluency	2 Maintenance	3 Generalization	COMMENTS
30	Makes socially acceptable comments about the physical appearance of communication partner	(ADULT)					
		(PEER)					
31	Uses words commensurate with developmental level	(ADULT)					
		(PEER)					
32	Uses conversation topics to discuss things happening at the time rather than perseverating on unrelated topics	(ADULT)					
		(PEER)					
33	Communicates anger/ frustration/disappointment in a non-aggressive manner	(ADULT)					
		(PEER)					
34	Engages in conversation by commenting on the previous statement and responding or elaborating	(ADULT)					
		(PEER)					
35	States a positive aspect of a situation	(ADULT)					
		(PEER)					
36	Introduces self to others	(ADULT)					
		(PEER)					

FSSA continued.

	UNDERSTANDING OF THE CONCEPT OF FRIENDSHIP	0 Acquisition	1 Fluency	2 Maintenance	3 Generalization	**COMMENTS**
1	Names one or more friends – identifies a person s/he knows as a friend					
2	Responds to compliments					
3	Tells why a specific person is their friend – shared activities/interests					
4	Refrains from teasing others					
5	Gives compliments, in a manner appropriate to developmental level and communication abilities					
6	Identifies characteristics or actions of a specific person who is not their friend					
7	Comments on important events in another's life ("Happy Birthday," "Congratulations/good job," "How was your trip/holiday?" etc.)					
8	Makes suggestions based on what someone else likes					
9	Demonstrates sensitivity to another person's needs by showing nonverbal/verbal concern when another is hurt					
10	Demonstrates sensitivity to another person's needs by offering help					

FSSA continued.

	UNDERSTANDING OF THE CONCEPT OF FRIENDSHIP	0 Acquisition	1 Fluency	2 Maintenance	3 Generalization	COMMENTS
11	Demonstrates sensitivity to another person's needs by offering consolation					
12	Gives verbal examples of ways people try to make friends					
13	Demonstrates that friendship is a positive reciprocal relationship (sharing a toy with someone who often shares with him/her; saving a seat for a friend who usually saves a seat for him/her)					
14	Changes actions, words, or tone in order to avoid hurting someone else					
15	Goes along with someone else's ideas, likes, opinions, and priorities that differ from his/her own					
16	Demonstrates that a disagreement doesn't need to end a friendship by interacting with a person in a positive way after a disagreement					
17	Identifies characteristics or actions of a specific person who is their friend versus someone who is just being polite					

FSSA continued.

	ENVIRONMENTAL REGULATION SKILLS	0 Acquisition	1 Fluency	2 Maintenance	3 Generalization	COMMENTS
1	Stays with adult when directed to					
2	Walks when inside buildings					
3	Uses an "inside voice"					
4	Keeps hands to self					
5	Carries own belongings					
6	Waits in line					
7	Follows posted rules					
8	Stays seated in vehicles					
9	Remains buckled in seat belt					
10	Keeps hands to self while riding in vehicles					
11	Refrains from distracting the driver					

FSSA continued.

	ENVIRONMENTAL REGULATION SKILLS	0 Acquisition	1 Fluency	2 Maintenance	3 Generalization	COMMENTS
12	Demonstrates safe behavior in and around parking lots					
13	Looks both ways for cars and crosses street when safe					
14	Refrains from speaking to strangers in the restroom					
15	Closes door when in restroom stall					
16	Removes only necessary clothing when using the restroom					
17	Remains in restroom for an appropriate period of time					
18	Adjusts clothing completely before leaving the restroom					
19	Washes hands after using the restroom					
20	Asks appropriate people for help when in community					
21	Relates to service personnel in a respectful manner					

FSSA continued.

	INDIVIDUAL IMPULSE CONTROL	0 Acquisition	1 Fluency	2 Maintenance	3 Generalization	**COMMENTS**
1	Waits for preferred item, activity, person for amount of time pre-determined by adult					
2	Follows the rules rather than acting on impulse (refrains from touching people, stays at table while eating, cleans up before moving to new activity)					
3	Demonstrates social behavior that is commensurate with developmental level while at functions such as parties/dances/pep-rallies/athletic events					
4	Manages responses to uncomfortable sensory experiences in a non-disruptive manner					
5	Accepts disappointment in a non-disruptive manner					

FSSA continued.

	MANNERS	0 Acquisition	1 Fluency	2 Maintenance	3 Generalization	COMMENTS
1	Keeps hands off of other people's food					
2	Takes appropriate-sized bites of food					
3	Covers mouth when sneezing, coughing, yawning					
4	Chews food with mouth closed					
5	Uses tissue to wipe nose					
6	Uses a napkin to wipe face and hands					
7	Uses utensils					
8	Waits until mouth is empty to begin talking					
9	Holds the door open for others					
10	Waits at table after eating until excused					
11	Offers people food on a plate when passing food					
12	When commenting on food, only makes positive statements					

FSSA continued.

	PERSONAL RESPONSIBILITY	0 Acquisition	1 Fluency	2 Maintenance	3 Generalization	COMMENTS
1	Accepts redirection from anyone in charge					
2	Apologizes in a manner commensurate with communication abilities					
3	Maintains personal hygiene					
4	Dresses to match occasion and weather					
5	When commenting about other people, only makes positive statements					
6	Uses an organizational technique to ensure having needed supplies in various situations					

	PROBLEM-SOLVING STRATEGIES	0 Acquisition	1 Fluency	2 Maintenance	3 Generalization	COMMENTS
1	Suggests taking turns					
2	Watches what others do and follows their example when appropriate					
3	Participates in and accepts group decisions					
4	Decides what another person wants and trades object or activity in order to obtain a desired object or activity					
5	Remembers and applies rules to problematic situations					
6	Compromises					
7	Asks for an impartial third person's opinion					

FSSA continued.

PLAY SKILLS	0 Acquisition	1 Fluency	2 Maintenance	3 Generalization	COMMENTS
1 Focuses on own activity					
2 Demonstrates awareness of others playing and looks to see what they are doing					
3 Plays independently but next to other children					
4 Demonstrates awareness of others playing and asks for something involved in the activity					
5 Follows a model					
6 Completes a short activity					
7 Cleans up activity					
8 Asks to join others in activity					
9 Takes turns					
10 Follows simple rules of a game					

FSSA continued.

	PLAY SKILLS	0 Acquisition	1 Fluency	2 Maintenance	3 Generalization	COMMENTS
11	Accepts clean-up time as a signal to stop playing without complaining					
12	Shares a preferred activity					
13	Asks another child to join in play					
14	Plays cooperatively with unfamiliar children					
15	Helps others					
16	Encourages others					
17	Initiates familiar play					
18	Demonstrates good sportsmanship after winning a game					
19	Communicates disappointment after losing a game in non-disruptive ways					

FSSA continued.

	READS, INTERPRETS AND RESPONDS TO SOCIAL CUES	0 Acquisition	1 Fluency	2 Maintenance	3 Generalization	COMMENTS
1	Acknowledges the presence of another person					
2	Repeats an activity in response to a positive reaction					
3	Discontinues an activity in response to a negative reaction					
4	Responds with rote social conventions (What do you say? = "please" or "thank you"; How are you? = "I'm fine. How are you?")					
5	Asks about another person's physical condition such as, "What did you do to your arm?"					
6	Asks about another person's feelings based on their facial expressions					
7	Asks for reasons for other people's feelings or emotions ("Why are you sad?")					

	RESPONDS TO INAPPROPRIATE SUGGESTIONS, REQUESTS, DARES	0 Acquisition	1 Fluency	2 Maintenance	3 Generalization	COMMENTS
1	Identifies characteristics or actions of a specific person who has bullied or who has taken advantage of them					
2	Uses planned, appropriate responses to teasing, dares, name calling, inappropriate requests or suggestions by bullies					
3	Communicates to an adult an understanding of inappropriate requests of a sexual nature from peers or adults in a manner commensurate to developmental level and communication abilities					
4	Uses proactive strategies to avoid potentially dangerous or uncomfortable situations (remains with a buddy, keeps doors open, makes an excuse to remove self from dangerous situation)					

FSSA continued.

	SELF-ADVOCACY SKILLS	0 Acquisition	1 Fluency	2 Maintenance	3 Generalization	COMMENTS
1	Expresses desires/preferences					
2	Asks for more					
3	Asks for help					
4	Tells appropriate people when hurt					
5	Refuses in a socially acceptable manner					
6	Asserts that it is his/her turn in a socially acceptable manner					
7	Asks permission to do what s/he wants to do					
8	Asks someone to move out of the way in a polite manner					
9	Communicates when proud of something					
10	Informs appropriate person when there is a problem (wrong food is served or something is broken)					
11	Asks for information					
12	Informs conversation partner when s/he was misunderstood					
13	Responds to criticism (asks for clarification, apologizes, asks for help)					

FSSA continued.

	TRANSITIONS	0 Acquisition	1 Fluency	2 Maintenance	3 Generalization	COMMENTS
1	Transitions from preferred to non-preferred people					
2	Transitions from familiar to non-familiar people					
3	Transitions from people s/he routinely sees to people who are seen unexpectedly					
4	Transitions from preferred to non-preferred activities and materials					
5	Transitions from familiar to non-familiar activities and materials					
6	Transitions from routine activities and materials to unexpected activities and materials					
7	Transitions from preferred to non-preferred locations					
8	Transitions from familiar to non-familiar locations					
9	Transitions from routine locations to unexpected locations					
10	Transitions from an unfinished activity to a new activity					
11	Asks questions about transitions ("What will we do?," "Will they have pizza to eat?," "Will it be noisy?")					

FSSA continued.

	WILLINGNESS TO DO NON-PREFERRED THINGS	0 Acquisition	1 Fluency	2 Maintenance	3 Generalization	COMMENTS
1	Tries new activities					
2	Visits new environments					
3	Interacts with new people					
4	Takes advice from others					
5	Tries new foods					
6	Re-visits non-preferred locations					

FSSA continued.

Note. A copy of the FSSA may be downloaded by the owner of this book from www.aapcpublishing.net/9106

The Visual Social Skills Profile

The Visual Social Skills Profile (VSSP) accompanies the FSSA and helps visually highlight where a student is functioning in social skills development. Specifically, the VSSP illustrates a student's current level of learning on each of the assessed social skills as well as the "splinter skills" that the student may have. This allows you to see at a glance the complete picture of the student's current social skills development as measured on the FSSA.

The VSSP consists of a set of concentric circles, with each circle representing one of the 13 skill areas on the FSSA, with the exception of the skill area Ability to Communicate Effectively With Communication Partner. As illustrated, this area consists of two concentric circles, one representing communication with an adult partner and the other representing communication with a peer.

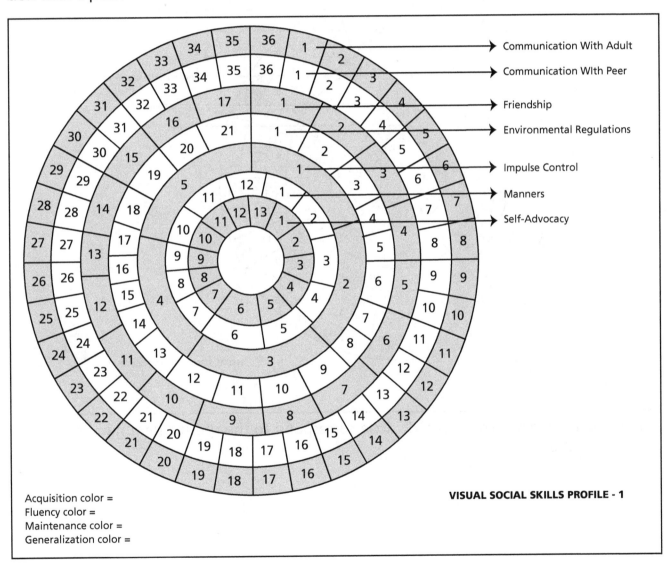

Communication With Adult
Communication With Peer
Friendship
Environmental Regulations
Impulse Control
Manners
Self-Advocacy

Acquisition color =
Fluency color =
Maintenance color =
Generalization color =

VISUAL SOCIAL SKILLS PROFILE - 1

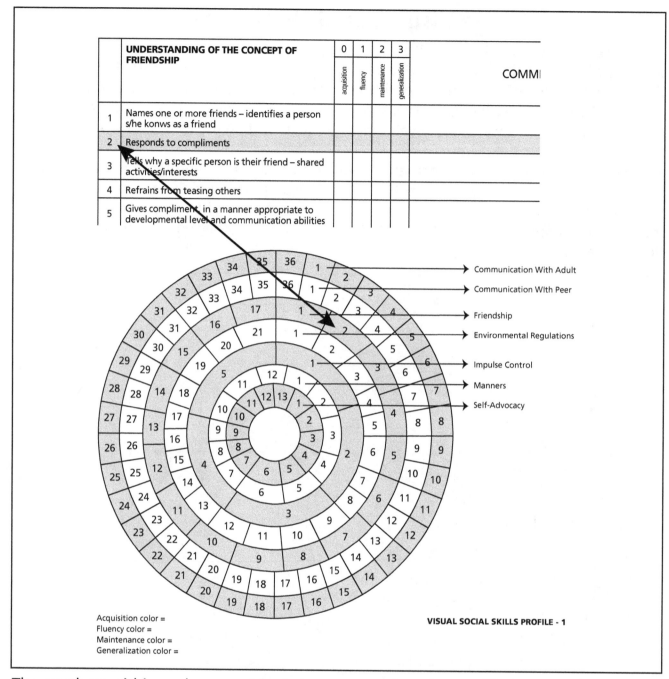

	UNDERSTANDING OF THE CONCEPT OF FRIENDSHIP	0	1	2	3	COMM...
		acquisition	fluency	maintenance	generalization	
1	Names one or more friends – identifies a person s/he konws as a friend					
2	Responds to compliments					
3	Tells why a specific person is their friend – shared activities/interests					
4	Refrains from teasing others					
5	Gives compliment in a manner appropriate to developmental level and communication abilities					

Communication With Adult
Communication WIth Peer
Friendship
Environmental Regulations
Impulse Control
Manners
Self-Advocacy

Acquisition color =
Fluency color =
Maintenance color =
Generalization color =

VISUAL SOCIAL SKILLS PROFILE - 1

The numbers within each concentric circle correspond to the specific item numbers on the FSSA within the skill area.

Directions for Completing the FSSA

1. Complete the FSSA for a specific student.

2. Select four different-colored pencils to represent the four levels of learning: acquisition, fluency, maintenance, and generalization. Indicate the colors you have chosen to use in the designated area at the bottom of the Visual Social Skills Profile.

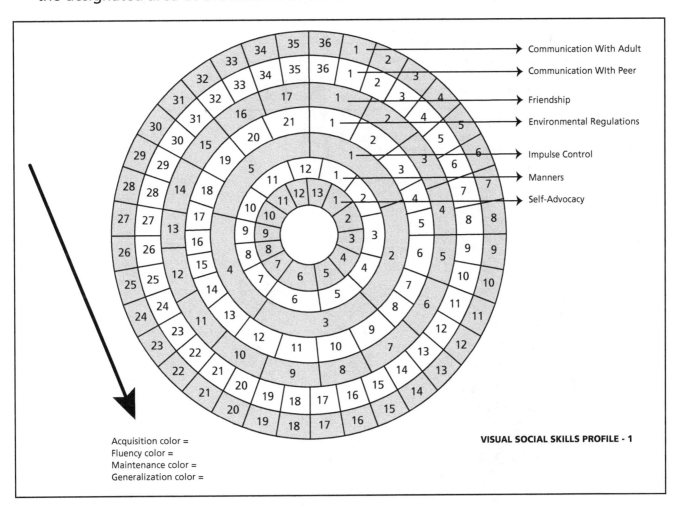

Communication With Adult

Communication With Peer

Friendship

Environmental Regulations

Impulse Control

Manners

Self-Advocacy

Acquisition color =
Fluency color =
Maintenance color =
Generalization color =

VISUAL SOCIAL SKILLS PROFILE - 1

3. Shade in the numbered arc on each of the concentric circles as you have scored the corresponding item on the FSSA using the color you have assigned to each of the levels of learning.

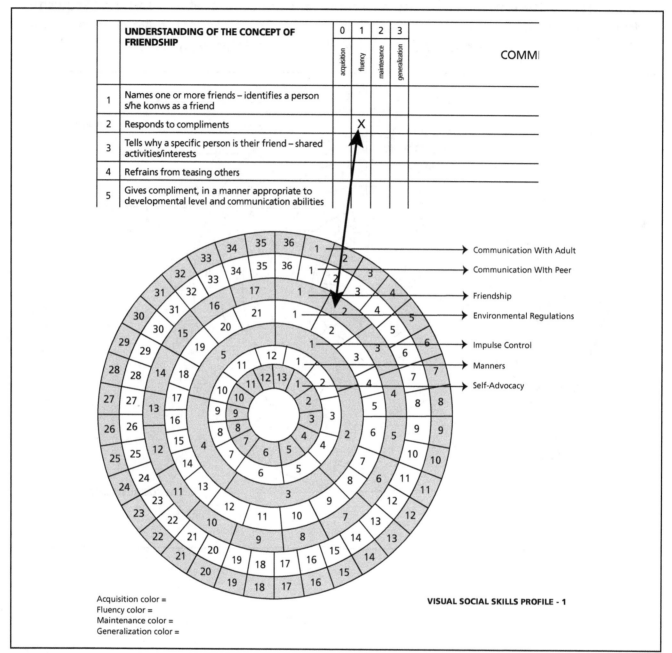

UNDERSTANDING OF THE CONCEPT OF FRIENDSHIP		0	1	2	3	
		acquisition	fluency	maintenance	generalization	COMMI
1	Names one or more friends – identifies a person s/he konws as a friend					
2	Responds to compliments		X			
3	Tells why a specific person is their friend – shared activities/interests					
4	Refrains from teasing others					
5	Gives compliment, in a manner appropriate to developmental level and communication abilities					

Communication With Adult
Communication With Peer
Friendship
Environmental Regulations
Impulse Control
Manners
Self-Advocacy

Acquisition color =
Fluency color =
Maintenance color =
Generalization color =

VISUAL SOCIAL SKILLS PROFILE - 1

4. Prioritize the skills identified in the FSSA that need to be taught. Write observable and measure IEP goals and objectives based on these skills.

5. Update the FSSA prior to the annual IEP meeting or when writing new social skills IEP goals and objectives. Use a new VSSP to record each year's information.

6. Attach the completed VSSP (the original profile and the updated profile) to the inside of a file folder. This enables you to display two years of growth in a side-by-side format.

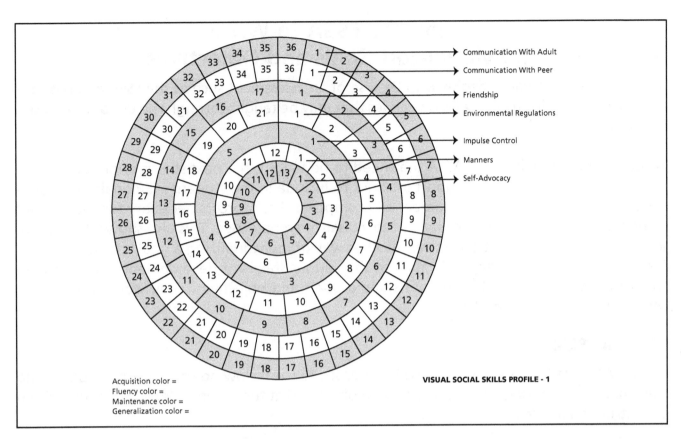

Communication With Adult
Communication With Peer
Friendship
Environmental Regulations
Impulse Control
Manners
Self-Advocacy

Acquisition color =
Fluency color =
Maintenance color =
Generalization color =

VISUAL SOCIAL SKILLS PROFILE - 1

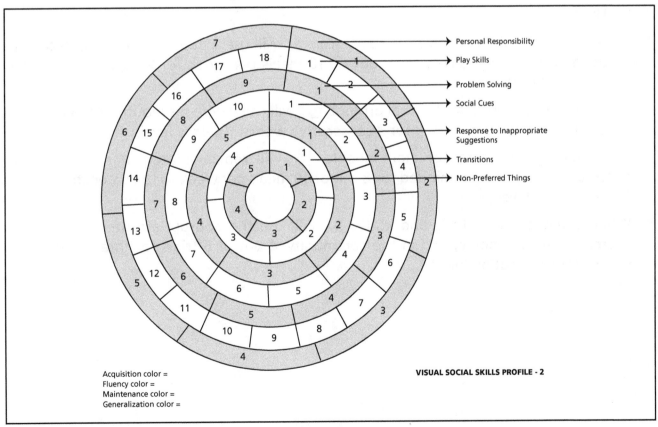

Personal Responsibility
Play Skills
Problem Solving
Social Cues
Response to Inappropriate Suggestions
Transitions
Non-Preferred Things

Acquisition color =
Fluency color =
Maintenance color =
Generalization color =

VISUAL SOCIAL SKILLS PROFILE - 2

Note. A copy of the VSSP may be downloaded by the owner of this book from www.aapcpublishing.net/9106

Using the FSSA to Write
Individualized Goals and Objectives

Social skills development begins with the use of an assessment such as the FSSA as a basis for writing individualized goals and objectives that may be taught through the use of the lessons in this program.

After identifying skills in the FSSA that need to be taught, the next step is prioritizing those skills and selecting the most important ones to include in the student's IEP goals and objectives. Specifying the type and number of prompts and reinforcers necessary for the student to demonstrate the skill is one way to individualize an objective. This also shows the level of learning obtained on that objective. Another way of individualizing a goal is by task analyzing a given skill and writing objectives at the various stages of development or accomplishment of the goal. The following are sample goals and objectives. They would need to be modified for a specific student.

Manners Skill Area

GOAL: When at the cafeteria, _____ will demonstrate the following socially acceptable eating behaviors by mastering 3 of the 4 following objectives at the criterion levels indicated within 36 instructional weeks.

OBJECTIVES:

1. When provided with a motivating reinforcer, ___ will use a napkin to wipe his face with verbal and gestural prompts for 5 out of 10 meals per week for 2 consecutive weeks. (acquisition level)

2. When given no more than 1 verbal prompt, ___ will chew with his mouth closed at school for 6 out of 10 meals per week for 3 consecutive weeks. (fluency level)

3. When eating with three or more people, ___ will remain seated at the table until excused without being reminded for 8 out of 10 meals per week for 2 consecutive weeks. (maintenance level)

4. When given a spoon, fork, and knife, ___ will use the appropriate utensil without a prompt at school, home, and in the community, 4 out of 5 trials for three consecutive weeks. (generalization level)

Communication Skill Area

GOAL: Within 36 instructional weeks, _____will respond when called by name by immediately stopping what he is doing and looking at the person speaking to him as evidenced by mastery of 3 of the following 4 objectives at the criterion levels stated.

OBJECTIVES:

1. When an adult is standing within 1 foot of the student, says his name very loudly, and taps him on the shoulder, ___ will stop whatever he is doing within 3 seconds, look at the adult, and receive a motivating reinforcer. This will be done 3 out of 4 times a day for 5 consecutive days. (acquisition)

2. When an adult is standing at least 3 feet away from the student and says his name very loudly, ___ will immediately stop whatever he is doing and look at the adult 3 out of 4 times a day for 5 consecutive days (fluency)

3. When an adult is standing at least 3 feet away from the student and says his name in a normal tone of voice, ___ will immediately stop whatever he is doing and look at the adult 3 out of 4 times a day for 15 consecutive days. (maintenance)

4. When any adult standing at least 3 feet away from the student says his name in a normal tone of voice, ___ will immediately stop whatever he is doing and look at the adult anywhere–at school, at home, or in the community–3 out of 4 times a day for 15 consecutive days. (generalization)

Willingness to Do Non-Preferred Things Area

GOAL: Within 36 instructional weeks, _____ will interact with at least one new person in a social situation as evidenced by mastery of the three following objectives at the criterion levels stated.

OBJECTIVES:

1. When in a familiar group of people in a social situation (e.g., lunch, recess) and asked, "Who would you like to show your (*favorite item/toy*) to?" ___ will identify one person he would like to show a favorite item/toy 2 out of 3 times asked.

2. When instructed to take an item/toy and stand next to or near the identified person, ___ will do so 3 out of 4 times when instructed.

3. When instructed to "Show him your (*favorite item/toy*)," _____ will do so 2 out of 3 times when instructed.

Putting It All Together

The following chart shows in which lessons each of the skill areas from the FSSA are taught. Use the chart to find the skill area in which a student is particularly weak and then make certain the lessons involving that skill area are stressed for that student.

	Meetings	Recess Treasure Hunt	Cooking Activity	Activities While Waiting	Games	Hidden Curriculum	Transitions	Doing Something Nice for Others	Show and Tell	Bullying
Ability to Communicate Effectively With Communication Partner (adults and peers)	X	X	X	X	X	X	X	X	X	X
Understanding of the Concept of Friendship	X	X			X	X		X	X	X
Environmental Regulation Skills	X		X	X	X	X	X			
Individual Impulse Control	X	X	X	X	X	X	X		X	X
Manners	X		X	X	X	X	X			
Personal Responsibility		X	X	X	X	X	X		X	
Play Skills		X		X	X	X			X	
Problem-Solving Strategies	X	X	X	X	X	X	X	X		X
Reads, Interprets, and Responds to Social Cues	X	X	X	X	X	X	X	X	X	X
Response to Inappropriate Suggestions, Requests, and Dares						X				X
Self-Advocacy Skills	X	X	X	X	X		X		X	X
Transitions		X	X	X			X		X	
Willingness to Do Non-Preferred Things		X	X	X	X	X	X	X	X	

EVIDENCE-BASED PRACTICES
USED IN THE LESSONS

The importance of using evidence-based practices (EBP) has become abundantly clear in recent years as a result of efforts by such organizations as the National Autism Center (www.nationalautismcenter.org). The following evidence-based strategies are referenced in the lessons in this program. Use and modify them to meet the needs of individual students, classrooms, and instructors.

Choice Making

Choice making is a strategy that has been shown effective as a means of increasing student participation and reducing challenging behaviors in a variety of settings and activities by allowing students an element of self-determination and control (Carter, 2001; Koegel, Werner, Vismara, & Koegel, 2005; Rogers, 2000). Choices relating to activities, reinforcers, materials, and participants can provide the motivation a student needs to engage in social, academic, and work activities, which also increases the likelihood of students demonstrating a desired behavior.

Choice-making opportunities should be tailored to students' individual cognitive, communication, and behavioral characteristics, and should only include options that the adult thinks are appropriate. Student choices can be expressed through verbal, pictorial, or augmentative communication means, and can be encouraged though the use of various forms of prompting or visual environmental supports. It is important that this strategy be implemented in the same way in all environments.

At Recess I Can:

Play in sandbox | Ask my friend to play tag | Climb on the jungle gym with the other kids

Errorless Learning

Errorless learning is an applied behavior analysis (ABA) strategy in which students are only provided with opportunities to learn a skill correctly (Alberto & Troutman, 2008; Polirstok, Dana, Buno, Mongelli, & Trubia, 2003). Instructors use various types of prompts and cues to ensure that errors do not occur. This strategy is especially effective with students who have difficulty understanding verbal directions, as only the desired and correct response is demonstrated. Errorless learning ensures that skills are taught in a way that minimizes frustration, increases the likelihood that only correct responses are repeated, and allows individuals to experience success even in the early phases of the learning process.

Fading

Fading is a strategy that originated with ABA (Alberto & Troutman, 2008). It is used to gradually increase a student's level of independence and proficiency in a given skill by systematically reducing the frequency and intrusiveness of prompts and cues. As students with autism often have difficulty generalizing skills, it is important to plan for the fading of supports prior to a skill being taught. Doing so will reduce the likelihood of the student becoming overly dependent on specific prompts or environmental, material, or personnel cues. Fading has been effectively used to teach social interaction skills to students with autism (Krantz & McClannahan, 1993, 1998).

Friends Teaching Friends

We are naturally drawn to people with whom we have things in common (Rubin, 2002). Often students with autism feel more comfortable and accepted by others whom they perceive to be similar to themselves. It is easier for a student to learn from a peer when that peer has similar types of interests and characteristics. These students can become friends who benefit from modeling for and learning from each other.

Friends Teaching Friends is at the heart of this program. Students on the autism spectrum benefit from learning from others socially, particularly from other students with autism. The comfort level and acceptance they can provide one another in social learning situations should not be underestimated. When they understand that there are other students with similar interests and characteristics, they begin to care about, listen to, and learn from these students, who often become their friends (Kluth & Schwarz, 2008).

Functional Routines (Rules and Routines)

Functional routines are daily occurrences that always happen at specific times and provide continuity, such as the use of a daily schedule (McClannahan & Krantz, 1999). They are often followed without a lot of thought, as students engage in the routine through habit. Consistent use of functional rules and routines helps students who have a need for sameness and predictability to feel comfortable. This, in turn, increases the likelihood of on-task, appropriate student behaviors, which is conducive to learning.

Rules and routines are most effective when conveyed in a positive manner that informs students of what they should be doing and when they should be doing it, such as greeting the teacher and classmates each morning (Krasny, Williams, Provencal, & Ozonoff, 2003). Further, rules and routines should be presented to students in the format that best corresponds to their cognitive and receptive communication skills, whether verbally, pictorially, or through the use of concrete objects.

Going Home Routine
1. Clean up area
2. Meet in "End of Day" circle – talk about what we learned
3. Get backpack and line up with bus riders
4. Walk with friends and teacher to bus
5. "Bye" to teacher
6. "Hi" to bus driver
7. Sit on bus

Joint Action Routines (JARS)

Joint action routines refer to specific procedures used to increase a student's spontaneous expressive communication and social communication skills and understanding (Snyder-McLean, Solomonson, McLean, & Sack, 1984). Routine interactions and the frequent repetition and practice of targeted language objectives are used in the context of activities that the student finds interesting or motivating. A typical situation for teaching using JARS with a student with classic autism involves the student saying, or otherwise indicating, "thank you," to the person serving the French fries at the cafeteria or waving goodbye to the driver when getting off the bus.

To be most effective, JARS should have meaningful themes, include an aspect of joint focus, have clearly defined roles for each participant, follow a predictable sequence, and be repeatable over time. Instructors should plan for generalization by preparing variations of the communicative exchange that the student can practice in the context of a known routine with different people or in different environments. JARS can be designed around an activity or task such as cooking, building a Lego® structure, or looking at the pictures in a book, or around cooperative activities and games that involve turn-taking.

Modeling

Modeling is a teaching procedure in which someone performs a task while a student watches. The student is then expected to follow this positive example. This might include watching another student get the basketball to go to P.E.; watching someone put materials away and get in line; or seeing a friend come in from recess, hang up his sweater, and take a chair to circle time.

An important prerequisite for successful modeling is that the student who is to learn by watching is able to focus on the other person, is interested in and understands what is happening, and has an opportunity to perform the task or behavior at a later time (Carr & Darcy, 1990; Siegel, 2003).

Picture Exchange Communication System

The Picture Exchange Communication System (PECS) is based on ABA techniques and is designed to make the most of the fact that many individuals with autism spectrum disorders are visual learners. The first step in the PECS procedure is to teach the student in a very concrete way that communication is an exchange between two or more people. Students with classic autism learn that they can get a favorite item by handing a picture of the item to a communication partner and immediately receiving the object in return. Functional communication is systematically taught using prompting and reinforcement strategies, eventually leading to independent communication.

> The PECS requires training to implement. Once the instructor is proficient with the system, the opportunities to increase a student's communication and social interaction skills are greatly expanded. One advantage of teaching the PECS protocol is that the use of pictures is a universally understood method of communicating with others (Bondy & Frost, 2002; Tincani & Devis, 2011).

Pivotal Response Training

Pivotal response training helps develop behaviors that are central to expanding a student's repertoire of skills, including social skills across environments (Koegel, 2012; Koegel & Frea, 1993). Pivotal behaviors include responding to multiple cues, developing motivation to initiate learning, self-management, and self-monitoring.

Students on the autism spectrum typically have difficulty generalizing skills and behaviors learned in one environment to another environment. By teaching a pivotal skill that can be used both at school and at home, generalization becomes easier. For example, a student may be taught at school to use multiple cues to discriminate among a variety of chairs of differing sizes and colors when the teacher asks him to look at a row of chairs and then sit in the small green chair. At home the child may be asked to use multiple cues to get his green shirt when there are a variety of shirts and sweaters in the closet. In both cases, the child is being taught to respond to multiple cues in a natural way.

Power Cards

Power Cards (Gagnon, 2001) are best used when the student has a specific and powerful interest in a person, object, or character that can be used to teach desired social behavior (Davis, Boon, Cihak, & Fore, 2010; Gagnon, 2001). When using Power Cards, a narrative is written from the perspective of the student's special interest (for example, Thomas the Tank Engine) that describes what the person or character would do in the same situation as the student is in. A card is created that summarizes the important things that the student should remember to do, and a picture of the special person or character is included. The card, which is often the size of a credit card, is carried as a reminder of the correct social behavior.

Gordon likes to be first out of the station. He knows his friends like to be first sometimes, too. When he gets upset about not being first, he can:

1. Ask the teacher when it is his turn to be first.

2. Keep track of whose turn it is to be first.

3. Find something special to do when he is last; like turning off the lights.

Priming

The purpose of priming is to familiarize students in a non-threatening and encouraging manner with the situations, procedures, and materials they will encounter. Priming should be individualized to a student's needs. It might be done through the use of pictures for very visual students, in a very brief session for students with classic autism who have a short attention span, or immediately prior to a social interaction for other students.

Priming can take place in a variety of settings, including at school by the teacher, at home by parents or siblings, or in the community by a social skills instructor. It should be a brief and positive experience for the student. Priming may include such activities as going over a student's object or picture schedule at the beginning of the school day, showing a student a picture to remind him to chew with his mouth closed before going to lunch, or preparing a student for a typical social situation in the gym (Sawyer, Luiselli, Ricciardi, & Gower, 2005; Zanolli, Daggett, & Adams, 1996).

Prompting

Prompting is an ABA strategy that is used to increase students' ability to independently perform any type of desired skill or behavior (Alberto & Troutman, 2008). Prompting assists in the acquisition of skills and behaviors by reinforcing students' successive approximations of the skills.

There are several types of prompting strategies, often used in a progression from least to most intrusive. For example, prompts may move from facial expressions to gestures to verbal reminders to physical guidance to hand-over-hand instruction. The prompts that are used when teaching a specific skill should be selected based on the student's current level of proficiency, cognitive abilities, and any behavioral or sensory characteristics that may be important. When prompts are used, it is important that a fading strategy be developed and implemented to prevent the student from becoming dependent on the additional assistance. The student learns to be more independent through the instructor's gradual withdrawal of the prompts.

Self-Monitoring Strategies –
Stress Thermometer, Incredible 5-Point Scale

Being aware of their emotions is important in all situations for students with autism. Stress thermometers are tools that help students understand when they are becoming stressed, when their behaviors are becoming increasingly intense or frequent, and how to manage such situations (Duncan & Klinger, 2010). By rating themselves on these visual scales, students can learn to identify, label, and regulate their emotions and behaviors and determine when they need a break, additional support, or even alone time.

The scales are particularly effective in that they show students visually how to indicate their level of stress or behavioral intensity.

The Incredible 5-Point Scale (Buron & Curtis, 2012) uses numbers to describe levels ranging from 1 to 5, with 5 describing the highest level of stress or problematic behavior. Many students on the autism spectrum have difficulty identifying in words how they are feeling. Being able to assign a number to their feelings helps students determine what to do based on learned strategies.

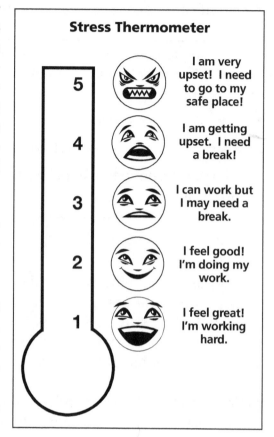

Stress Thermometer

5 — I am very upset! I need to go to my safe place!

4 — I am getting upset. I need a break!

3 — I can work but I may need a break.

2 — I feel good! I'm doing my work.

1 — I feel great! I'm working hard.

Shaping

Shaping is a part of the principles of ABA (Alberto & Troutman, 2008). It is used when the student needs to learn a new behavior, when an existing behavior needs to be changed or modified, or when the student exhibits only a portion of the desired behavior and needs to learn the rest. The strategy involves reinforcing successive approximations of a desired behavior. If a student is asked to go to her seat, for example, a reinforcer would be given for turning in the direction of the seat, and steps taken toward the seat would be reinforced until the student has completed the request. This strategy allows for administering reinforcement even before the entire task is mastered. This is especially important for students on the autism spectrum, many of whom need a high level and frequency of reinforcement to remain focused and accomplish a task or desired behavior.

A high level of reinforcement is particularly needed in the acquisition stage of learning in order to communicate to the student when the correct approximations are being made toward the desired behavior. In addition, reinforcement is needed to encourage the student to continue in the learning process when the final result may be a long way off. The strategy requires that the teacher knows and can clearly define each step of the desired behavior. It also requires that the teacher knows the student's reinforcers and how to administer them in a timely and effective manner.

Social Autopsies

A social autopsy (Lavoie, cited in Bieber, 1994) is used after a problematic inappropriate social interaction. It gives the adult and student a positive, productive means of analyzing what happened during the interaction or the social error. It can be implemented in a variety of ways, all of which focus on how the student can have a more successful interaction the next time. Thus, social autopsies are carried out in a nonjudgmental way by focusing on what to do in the future rather than assigning blame.

The strategy requires that the student is able to understand and verbalize what happened during the incident. It is best implemented by an adult whom the student trusts and to whom she can relate. It's important that the adult understand the student. Lavoie (cited in Bieber, 1994) suggested that the procedure include all people involved in the specific incident. For an example, see page 143.

Social Narratives

Social narratives are used in various ways, depending on the needs of the student, the student's level of functioning, and the social situation. Social narratives have the following characteristics:

1. They address a social situation with which the student is having difficulty.

2. They are individualized to the student's situation, needs, and cognitive level.

3. The narrative and visuals, if used, are written by the adult and address the specific situation using the student's name and other personalized information.

4. The narrative is read to and with the student. The student practices the strategies suggested in the narrative.

5. The narrative is used before potential problematic social situations occur to help prepare the student. (Myles & Simpson, 2003; Myles, Trautman, & Schelvan, 2013)

Social Scripts

A social script is a written statement that gives the student ideas about specific things that might be said in a social situation (Stevenson, Krantz, & McClannahan, 2000; Wichnick, Vener, Keating, & Poulson, 2009). Students who have difficulties initiating communication or generating language benefit from social scripts. Students memorize the social script and learn when and how to use it appropriately. This builds confidence and increases the likelihood of a successful social experience.

Teaching at the Point of Performance

Teaching at the point of performance is a foundation for this social skills program. This term was first used by Dr. Sam Goldstein to describe the critical place and time for performing a task (Barkley, 2000; Brooks & Goldstein, 2012). The strategy addresses many of the basic needs of students with classic autism, who often have difficulty with generalization because they do not apply previously learned information and skills when and where needed – at the point of performance. Another value of teaching at the point of performance is the built-in motivation to use a skill while participating in a favorite activity. Additionally, this strategy helps instructors diagnose some of the subtle skills and behaviors that students with classic autism have not learned and do not use in real-life situations.

Teaching at the point of performance occurs when instructors make use of typical, everyday events that occur in natural settings for teaching, practicing, and refining needed skills and as a way of motivating students to participate in these opportunities. Students are taught specific skills in order to prepare them prior to going into a new setting and are encouraged to practice and build on these skills in the situations and settings in which they need to be used. Errors are treated as teachable moments and are handled as they occur in a calm and instructive manner.

Using Students' Special Interests

Individuals with classic autism are frequently interested in and motivated by very specific items, activities, topics, or sensations. These special interests can be used effectively as teaching materials, reinforcers after specific skills or behaviors are demonstrated, and as a means of encouraging students to participate in important but non-preferred activities or tasks (Baker, 2000; Grandin, 2008; Kluth & Schwarz, 2008; Mesibov, 1998).

Teaching through special interests is a way of using what is viewed as one of the challenging characteristics of autism, the stereotyped patterns of behavior and restricted interests, in a positive way that can lead to growth in a variety of skill areas. For example, some students may be willing to engage with others in a social setting if given the opportunity to discuss topics of interest to them, while others are better able to tolerate being in new or unfamiliar environments if allowed to bring a favorite item.

Visual Environmental Supports

Most students with autism spectrum disorders are visual learners and have a need for structure, organization, consistency, and predictability. Visual supports present specific information in a way that can meet all of these needs.

Information presented in a visual format may be the class schedule, a student's individual daily schedule, behavioral expectations, steps in a daily living skill, suggested rules for a social interaction, and steps required to complete an academic task. Visual supports are individualized to meet the student's physical needs regarding the size and placement of the visual information and the student's cognitive needs regarding the appropriate level of abstraction from concrete objects, to photographs, line drawings, icons and/or words (Johnston, Nelson, Evans, & Palazolo, 2003; Machalicek et al., 2009; Mesibov, Shea, & Schopler, 2005).

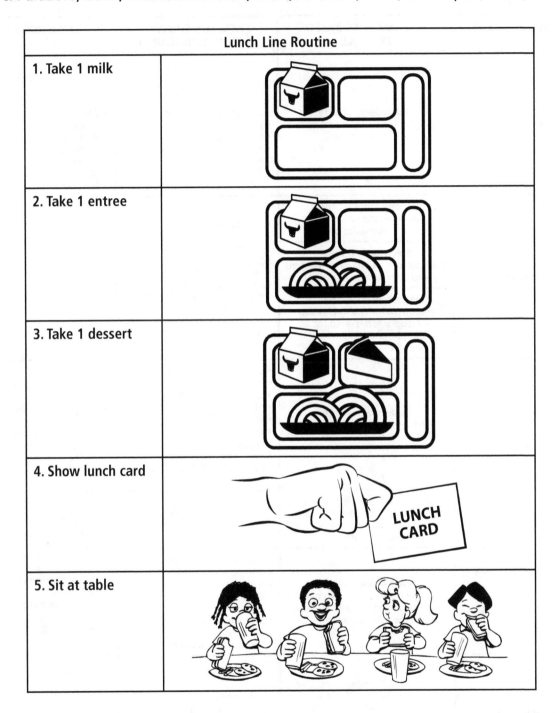

Lunch Line Routine	
1. Take 1 milk	
2. Take 1 entree	
3. Take 1 dessert	
4. Show lunch card	
5. Sit at table	

EVIDENCE BASED PRACTICES FOUND IN THE NATIONAL AUTISM CENTER'S AUTISM IN THE SCHOOLS GUIDE CORRELATED WITH TEACHING STRATEGIES FOUND IN TEACHING FUNCTIONAL SOCIAL SKILLS IN NATURAL SETTINGS			
TEACHING STRATEGY	**NAC EVIDENCE-BASED PRACTICE**	**BENEFITS SHOWN THROUGH RESEARCH**	**RECOMMENDED LESSONS FOR USE**
Choice Making	**Antecedent Package** (changing the environment before a behavior occurs)	• communication skills • interpersonal skills • personal responsibility • play skills • self-regulation • sensory and emotional regulation	• Meetings • Recess Treasure Hunt • Cooking Activity • Activities While Waiting • Games • Hidden Curriculum • Transitions • Doing Something Nice for Others • Show and Tell • Bullying
Errorless Learning	**Antecedent Package** (changes in the environment before a behavior occurs) **Behavioral Package** (changes in the environment before and after a behavior occurs) **Comprehensive Behavioral Treatment for Young Children** (programs designed for early intervention to help young children with ASD)	• communication skills • interpersonal skills • personal responsibility • play skills • self-regulation • restricted, repetitive nonfunctional patterns of behavior • sensory and emotional regulation	• Games • Bullying
Fading	**Behavioral Package** (changes in the environment before and after a behavior occurs)	• communication skills • interpersonal skills • personal responsibility • play skills • self-regulation • sensory and emotional regulation • restricted, repetitive, nonfunctional patterns of behavior	• Meetings • Recess Treasure Hunt • Cooking Activity • Activities While Waiting • Games • Hidden Curriculum • Doing Something Nice for Others • Show and Tell • Bullying
Friends Teaching Friends	**Joint Attention Intervention** (individuals focusing at the same time on an object and/or activity and each other) **Peer Training Package** (training peers in how to have positive interactions with students on the autism spectrum)	• communication skills • interpersonal skills • communication skills • interpersonal skills • play skills • social interaction • sharing • offering and seeking assistance • being a "good buddy"	• Meetings • Recess Treasure Hunt • Cooking Activity • Activities While Waiting • Games • Hidden Curriculum • Transitions • Doing Something Nice for Others • Show are Tell
Functional Routines	**Naturalistic Teaching Strategies** (using a variety of natural materials together with direct and natural consequences to motivate students, with the goal of generalizing relevant skills)	• communication skills • interpersonal skills • generalization • play skills	• Meetings • Cooking Activity • Activities While Waiting • Games • Hidden Curriculum • Transitions • Doing Something Nice for Others • Show and Tell

TEACHING STRATEGY	NAC EVIDENCE-BASED PRACTICE	BENEFITS SHOWN THROUGH RESEARCH	RECOMMENDED LESSONS FOR USE
Joint Action Routines (JARS)	**Joint Attention Intervention** (people focusing at the same time on an object and/or activity and each other)	• communication skills • interpersonal skills	• Meetings • Recess Treasure Hunt • Cooking Activity • Activities While Waiting • Games • Show and Tell
Modeling	Modeling (showing how to do something after gaining the student's attention)	• communication skills • interpersonal skills • personal responsibility • play skills • problem behaviors • sensory and emotional regulation	• Meetings • Recess Treasure Hunt • Cooking Activity • Activities While Waiting • Games • Hidden Curriculum • Transitions • Doing Something Nice for Others • Show and Tell
Picture Exchange Communication System (PECS)	**Behavioral Package** (changes in the environment before and after a behavior occurs)	• communication skills • interpersonal skills • play skills • self-regulation • sensory and emotional regulation	• Meetings • Recess Treasure Hunt • Cooking Activity • Activities While Waiting • Games • Show and Tell
Power Cards	**Story-Based Interventions** (increasing perspective-taking skills through stories written from the perspective of a favorite person/character that include information about the who/what/when/where/why of a target behavior)	• communication skills • interpersonal skills • understanding emotions • making choices • mealtime skills • play skills • problem behaviors • self-regulation	• Games • Transitions • Bullying
Priming	**Antecedent Package** (changes in the environment before a behavior occurs)	• communication skills • interpersonal skills • personal responsibility • play skills • self-regulation • sensory and emotional regulation	• Meetings • Recess Treasure Hunt • Cooking Activity • Activities While Waiting • Games • Hidden Curriculum • Transitions • Doing Something Nice for Others • Show and Tell • Bullying
Prompting	**Antecedent Package** (changes in the environment before a behavior occurs)	• communication skills • interpersonal skills • personal responsibility • play skills • self-regulation • sensory and emotional regulation	• Meetings • Recess Treasure Hunt • Cooking Activity • Activities While Waiting • Games • Hidden Curriculum • Transitions • Doing Something Nice for Others • Show and Tell • Bullying
Self-Monitoring Strategies – Stress Thermometer, The Incredible 5-Point Scale	**Self-Management** (selecting reinforcers, monitoring and evaluating one's own performance, and independently gaining access to reinforcers)	• interpersonal skills • self-regulation	• Games • Transitions • Bullying

TEACHING STRATEGY	NAC EVIDENCE-BASED PRACTICE	BENEFITS SHOWN THROUGH RESEARCH	RECOMMENDED LESSONS FOR USE
Shaping	**Behavioral Package** (changes in the environment before and after a behavior occurs)	• communication skills • interpersonal skills • personal responsibility • play skills • restricted, repetitive, nonfunctional patterns of behavior • self-regulation • sensory and emotional regulation	• Meetings • Recess Treasure Hunt • Activities While Waiting • Games • Hidden Curriculum • Doing Something Nice for Others • Show and Tell • Bullying
Social Autopsies	no equivalent strategy listed in the National Autism Center's Evidence-Based Practice and Autism in the Schools guide		• Games • Hidden Curriculum • Bullying
Social Narratives	**Story-Based Interventions** (increasing perspective-taking skills through stories written from an "I" or "some people" perspective that include information about the who/what/when/where/why of a target behavior)	• communication skills • interpersonal skills • understanding emotions • making choices • mealtime skills • play skills • problem behaviors • self-regulation	• Meetings • Recess Treasure Hunt • Cooking Activity • Activities While Waiting • Games • Hidden Curriculum • Transitions • Doing Something Nice • Show and Tell • Bullying
Social Scripts	**Antecedent Package** (changes in the environment before a behavior occurs)	• communication skills • interpersonal skills • personal responsibility • play skills • self-regulation • sensory and emotional regulation	• Meetings • Recess Treasure Hunt • Cooking Activity • Activities While Waiting • Games • Show and Tell • Bullying
Teaching at the Point of Performance	**Naturalistic Teaching Strategies** (using a variety of natural materials together with direct and natural consequences to motivate students, with the goal of generalizing relevant skills)	• communication skills • interpersonal skills • generalization • play skills	• Meetings • Recess Treasure Hunt • Cooking Activity • Activities While Waiting • Games • Hidden Curriculum • Transitions • Doing Something Nice for Others • Show and Tell • Bullying
Using Students' Special Interests	**Antecedent Package** (changes in the environment before a behavior occurs)	• communication skills • interpersonal skills • personal responsibility • play skills • self-regulation • sensory and emotional regulation	• Meetings • Recess Treasure Hunt • Activities While Waiting • Games • Doing Something Nice for Others • Show and Tell
Visual Environmental Supports	**Schedules** (promoting greater independence and managing transitions by enhancing student's ability to predict future events through advance planning)	• problematic behaviors • self-regulation	• Meetings • Recess Treasure Hunt • Cooking Activity • Activities While Waiting • Games • Hidden Curriculum • Transitions • Doing Something Nice • Show and Tell • Bullying

References and Resources

Alberto, P. A., & Troutman, A. G. (2008). *Applied behavior analysis for teachers* (8th ed.). Columbus, OH: Merrill Prentice Hall.

Baker, M. J. (2000). Incorporating the thematic ritualistic behavior of children with autism into games: Increasing social play interactions with siblings. *Journal of Positive Behavior Interventions, 2,* 66-84.

Barkley, R. (2000). *Taking charge of ADHD.* New York, NY: Guilford Press.

Bieber, J. (1994). *Learning disabilities and social skills with Richard Lavoie: Last one picked ... first one picked on.* Washington, DC: Public Broadcasting Service.

Bondy, A., & Frost, L. (2002). *A picture's worth: PECS and other visual communication strategies in autism (Topics in Autism).* Bethesda, MD: Woodbine House.

Brooks, R., & Goldstein, S. (2012). *Raising resilient children with autism spectrum disorders: Strategies for helping them maximize their strengths, cope with adversity, and develop a social mindset.* New York, NY: McGraw Hill.

Carr, E. G., & Darcy, M. (1990). Setting generality of peer modeling in children with autism. *Journal of Autism and Developmental Disorders, 20*(1), 45-59.

Carter, C. M. (2001). Using choice with game play to increase language skills and interactive behaviors in children with autism. *Journal of Positive Behavioral Intervention, 3*(3), 131-151.

Davis, K. M., Boon, R. T., Cihak, D. F., & Fore III, C. (2010). Power cards to improve conversational skills in adolescents with Asperger syndrome. *Focus on Autism and other Developmental Disabilities, 25*(1), 12-22.

Duncan, A., & Klinger, L. (2010). Autism spectrum disorders: Building social skills in group, school and community settings. *Social Work with Groups: A Journal of Community and Clinical Practice, 33*(2-3), 175-193.

Gagnon, E. (2001). *Power Cards: Using special interests to motivate children and youth with Asperger syndrome and autism.* Shawnee Mission, KS: AAPC Publishing.

Grandin, T. (2008). *The way I see it: A personal look at autism & Asperger's.* Arlington, TX: Future Horizons.

Johnston, S., Nelson, C., Evans, J., & Palazolo, K. (2003). The use of visual supports in teaching young children with autism spectrum disorder to initiate interaction. *Augmentative and Alternative Communication, 19,* 86-103.

Kluth, P., & Schwarz, P. (2008). *"Just give him the whale!" 20 ways to use fascinations, areas of expertise, and strengths to support students with autism.* Baltimore, MD: Paul H. Brookes Publishing Company.

Koegel, L. (2012). *Pivotal response treatments: Improving socialization in individuals with autism.* Santa Barbara, CA: Behavior Management Student Organization.

Koegel, R., & Frea, W. (1993). Treatment of social behavior in autism through the modification of pivotal social skills. *Journal of Applied Behavior Analysis, 26,* 369-377.

Koegel, R. L., Werner, G. A., Vismara, L. A., & Koegel, L. K. (2005). The effectiveness of contextually supported play-based interactions between children with autism and typically developing peers. *Research and Practice for Persons with Severe Disabilities, 30*(2), 93-102.

Krantz, P. J., & McClannahan, L. (1993). Teaching children with autism to initiate to peers: Effects of a script-fading procedure. *Journal of Applied Behavior Analysis, 26,* 121-132.

Krantz, P. J., & McClannahan, L. (1998). Social interaction skills for children with autism: A script fading procedure for beginning readers. *Journal of Applied Behavior Analysis, 31*(2), 191-202.

Krasny, L., Williams, B. J., Provencal, S., & Ozonoff, S. (2003). Social skills intervention for the autism spectrum: Essential ingredients in a model curriculum. *Child and Adolescent Psychiatric Clinics of North America, 12*(1), 107-122.

Machalicek, W., Shogren, K., Lang, R., Rispoli, M., O'Reilly, M. F., Franko, J. H., & Sigafoos, J. (2009). Increasing play and decreasing the challenging behavior of children with autism during recess with activity schedules and task correspondent training. *Research in Autism Spectrum Disorders, 3*(2), 547-555.

McClannahan, L. E., & Krantz, P. J. (1999). *Activity schedules for children with autism: Teaching independent behavior.* Bethesda, MD: Woodbine House.

Mesibov, G. B. (1998). Editorial. *Journal of Autism and Developmental Disorders, 28*(6), 465-466.

Mesibov, G. B., Shea, V., & Schopler, E. (2005). *The TEACCH approach to autism spectrum disorders.* New York, NY: Plenum Press.

Myles, B. S., & Simpson, R. L. (2003). *Asperger Syndrome: A guide for educators and parents* (2nd ed.). Austin, TX: Pro-Ed.

Myles, B. S., Trautman, M. L., & Schelvan, R. L. (2013). *The hidden curriculum for understanding unstated rules in social situations for adolescents and young adults.* Shawnee Mission, KS: AAPC Publishing.

Orsmond, G. I., Krauss, M. W., & Seltzer, M. M. (2004). Peer relationships and social and recreational activities among adolescents and adults with autism. *Journal of Autism and Developmental Disabilities, 34*(3), 245-256.

Polirstok, S. R., Dana, L., Buno, S. D., Mongelli, V. D., & Trubia, G. D. (2003). Improving functional communication skills in adolescents and young adults with severe autism using gentle teaching and positive approaches. *Topics in Language Disorders, 23*(2), 146-153.

Rogers, S. J. (2000). Interventions that facilitate socialization in children with autism. *Journal of Autism and Developmental Disorders, 30*(5), 399-409.

Rubin, K. H. (2002). *The friendship factor.* New York, NY: Viking Penguin.

Sawyer, L., Luiselli, J., Ricciardi, J., & Gower, J. (2005). Teaching a child with autism to share among peers in an integrated pre-school classroom: Acquisition, maintenance and social validation. *Education and Treatment of Children, 28,*1-10.

Siegel, B. (2003). *Helping children with autism learn.* New York, NY: Oxford University Press, Inc.

Snyder-McLean, L., Solomonson, B., McLean, J., & Sack, S. (1984). Structuring joint action routines: A strategy for facilitating communication and language development in the classroom. *Seminars in Speech and Language, 5,* 213-228.

Stevenson, C. L., Krantz, T .J., & McClannahan, L. E. (2000). Social interaction skills for children with autism: A script fading procedure for non-readers. *Behavioral Intervention, 15,* 1-20.

Tincani, M., & Devis, K. (2011). Quantitative synthesis and component analysis of single-participant studies on the picture exchange communication system. *Remedial & Special Education, 32*(6), 458-470.

Wichnick, A. M., Vener, S. M., Keating, C., & Poulson, C. L. (2009). The effect of a script fading procedure on unscripted social initiations and novel utterances of young children with autism. *Research in Autism Spectrum Disorders, 4,* 51-64.

Zanolli, K., Daggett, J., & Adams, T. (1996). Teaching preschool age autistic children to make spontaneous initiations to peers using priming. *Journal of Autism and Developmental Disorders, 26*(4), 407-422.

COMPREHENSIVE AUTISM PLANNING SYSTEM (CAPS)

When working with students with classic autism, it is extremely important to individualize for the specific needs and characteristics of each student. One convenient tool for doing this is Shawn Henry and Brenda Smith Myles' Comprehensive Autism Planning System (CAPS; 2013).

The CAPS is designed to provide an overview of a student's daily schedule by time and activity as well as the supports the student needs during each period. Everybody who works with a given student contributes to the development of the CAPS.

The following CAPS chart addresses the areas that should be considered when planning and teaching each of the following lessons. Specifically, Time, Activity, Targeted Skills to Teach, Structure/Modifications, Reinforcement, Sensory Strategies, Communication/Social Skills, Data Collection, and Generalization Plan.

Student: _____   **Age:** _____

Comprehensive Autism Planning System (CAPS)

Time	Activity	Targeted Skills to Teach	Structure/ Modifications	Reinforcement	Sensory Strategies	Communication/ Social Skills	Data Collection	Generalization Plan

From Henry, S. A., & Myles, B. S. (2013). *The Comprehensive Autism Planning System (CAPS) for Individuals With Autism Spectrum Disorders and Related Disabilities* (2nd ed.). Shawnee Mission, KS: AAPC Publishing. www.aapcpublishing.net; used with permission.

Comprehensive Autism Planning System (CAPS) - EXAMPLE

Student: Sarah (served in a self-contained setting, has some expressive language but also uses PECS notebook)   **Age: 9**

Time	Activity	Targeted Skills to Teach	Structure/ Modifications	Reinforcement	Sensory Strategies	Communication/ Social Skills	Data Collection	Generalization Plan
11:45-12:15	Lunch	Responds to greetings	– practice in classroom using a pictorial social script – ask adults in cafeteria to greet Sarah each day – prompt if needed – fading	– smiles, high-5's from others – verbal praise		– accept either waving or saying, "Hi!"	– record number and level of prompts needed	– practice responding to greetings from a variety of people at natural opportunities throughout the day
		Uses napkin to wipe face and hands	– pictorial first/ then board (first = eat, then = use napkin) – ask peer to model napkin use	– verbal praise – token on board for each time napkin is used (5 tokens = 5 minutes on iPad after lunch)			– frequency count number of times napkin is used	– share strategies with parents for use at home
		Responds when given a choice – select desired food in cafeteria line	– review lunch choices prior to leaving class (priming) – pictures of lunch choices in PECS notebook	– desired food items – verbal praise – thank her for letting others know what she wants to eat		– accept verbal requests for food or PECS	– record if choices were made	– offer choices throughout the day in a variety of school settings
		Manages responses to uncomfortable sensory experiences in a non-disruptive manner – noise in cafeteria	– use 5-Point Scale on noise level in cafeteria		– allow to swing in motor room for 5 minutes prior to lunch – noise cancelling head phones available for use in cafeteria			

LESSONS

Meetings

Purpose

Many students with classic autism have difficulty participating in group activities (Gerberding, 2007). This lesson is designed to motivate students to take part in one type of group activity. Through participation students learn needed social skills and practice generalizing them.

This activity is intentionally called a "meeting." This distinguishes the activity from the usual classroom circle time, and for older students makes it more age-appropriate and adult-like. The meeting is different also because it follows specific and purposeful routines geared toward social skill development established by the teacher in response to the needs of the students. The students learn to interact with each other in a positive way, and are motivated to gradually build on and generalize this fundamental skill through more sophisticated interactions. Some student interactions occur naturally whereas others are arranged by the teacher.

Targeted Skill Categories From the FSSA

Look at the list of skill categories below and determine if any of them pose a need for your students. For example, you may have students who never participate in group activities because they don't share information when asked (Ability to Communicate Effectively With Communication Partner), very seldom receive or respond appropriately to compliments from peers (Understanding of the Concept of Friendship), or find it difficult to maintain personal space (Individual Impulse Control). This is a good lesson for these students.

- Ability to Communicate Effectively With Communication Partner
- Environmental Regulation Skills
- Individual Impulse Control
- Manners
- Problem-Solving Strategies
- Reads, Interprets, and Responds to Social Cues
- Self-Advocacy Skills
- Understanding of the Concept of Friendship

Recommended Evidence-Based Practices

The following evidence-based practices are recommended for this lesson.

- Choice Making
- Fading
- Friends Teaching Friends
- Functional Routines (Rules and Routines)
- Joint Action Routines (JARS)
- Modeling
- Picture Exchange Communication System (PECS)
- Pivotal Response Training
- Priming
- Prompting
- Shaping
- Social Narratives
- Social Scripts
- Teaching at the Point of Performance
- Using Special Interests
- Visual Environmental Supports

Considerations for This Lesson

Meetings provide opportunities for developing many social skills for students with classic autism because they offer both a structured agenda and also variation within that agenda. For example, a typical meeting agenda may be as follows: (a) everyone takes a turn sharing one good thing that has happened since the last meeting; (b) everyone gives a compliment to someone attending the meeting; and (c) the meeting ends with an age- and ability- appropriate motivating game, such as "20 Questions," *UNO*®, or *Bingo*®, modified to the extent necessary for everyone to participate and have fun.

The social skills instructor must be familiar with each student's social skills goals and objectives. It is not necessary that all students work on the same goals and objectives or are at the same level of learning. In fact, it is sometimes easier if students are at different levels and able to help each other. One student may be at the acquisition level in "giving a compliment" whereas another student might be at the generalization level. Expectations, cues, reinforcers, and interactions would be different for these two students. The student who has mastered giving a compliment will have an opportunity to practice other goals and objectives, such as listening to a friend or waiting. Other students may have the opportunity to generalize their abilities by teaching or modeling for another class member.

Many different goals and objectives may be addressed simultaneously during a meeting, depending on the needs of the individual students. This does not mean that each student's FSSA or IEP needs to be memorized. However, the instructor must be familiar with how each student's needs and abilities fit into the plans developed for a given day's meeting.

Materials

The following materials are optional. Materials selection depends mainly on the age and ability levels of the students involved in the meeting.

- Pictorial guidelines for meetings

- A game to play at the end of the meeting

- A snack if this is to be part of the meeting. It is often a good idea to include an easy snack that the students make (i.e., frost 'Nilla Wafers, peanut butter on crackers, stirring chocolate into milk, individual microwaveable Brownie Bowls®, etc.) as one of the routines in the meeting. Note: Many students on the autism spectrum have food allergies or other dietary restrictions. This must be checked before using any food in the classroom.

- Books (joke books, a book that goes along with whatever topic or lesson you are emphasizing in the meeting, a special interest book to share with one participant who tells the others about the book, etc.).

- *The Hidden Curriculum* by Brenda Smith Myles et al. (2013) is a guide for recognizing and teaching "unwritten social rules," which people with classic autism often do not know or understand. One of these unwritten social rules is *not announcing to the group when one has to use the restroom*. Another social rule might be *not to say something unkind about another person's appearance*.

- Anything that "sets the atmosphere" for the meeting, such as a quiet corner with special lighting, comfortable seating, or other environmental indications that this is an informal social activity.

Steps in Implementing This Lesson

1. Select target social skills to address during the meeting. This does not mean teaching these skills in a discrete lesson format, but addressing them as they occur naturally when the students interact during the meeting. The philosophy of this program is to teach skills in context as they are needed. Therefore, the compliments, explanations, redirections, and corrections depend on the individual students' levels of understanding, skills, and motivators.

2. Have the meeting area and materials organized and ready for students.

3. Encourage routines to develop over time based on the nature and personalities of the students and the dynamics of the group.

4. Increase expectations for social skills and interactions as the students gain competence and skills.

5. Develop positive and motivating ways to encourage participation from reluctant students. This may involve incorporating natural reinforcers into the meeting format, such as adding a snack, discussing a favorite topic, or encouraging other group members to act as mentors.

Sample Activities in a Meeting for Students Who Are Nonverbal

- Make the meeting shorter and the students more physically active. The objectives will be limited. More visual supports will be needed.

- Expect all students to "say" something to each other. This might involve having a student wave and say "hi" or the equivalent to each group member. Perhaps a student could point to another student's shoes, socks, shirt, or toy car after the instructor says, "Matthew likes Johnny's …"

- Have students bring a favorite item to share.

- Play group game such as throwing *UNO* cards into a box.

- Use pictures/objects to prepare for an upcoming event.

Extension Activities for Students Who Are Higher Functioning

- Introduce a theme for the meeting discussion such as "My Favorite TV Program," "My Favorite Music," and/or "Things I Like to Do on Saturday." As the students find things they have in common, often new or deepened friendships occur. Students who are limited verbally could get help when others ask them questions regarding the topic and they indicate their responses nonverbally with communication devices or by reaching for or pointing to a favorite object or picture.

- Invite a favorite guest to join the meeting and participate by answering questions and discussing the topic of the day. This might be the principal, another teacher, or a peer from a general education class.

Extensions for Parents

Encourage and work with parents to do any or all of the following:
- Incorporate a social routine into dinnertime by having everyone say one good thing that happened to them that day.

- During holiday meals, start or continue a family tradition whereby each person names one thing he or she is grateful for.

- Hold a family meeting each week where every member gives input on what movie they will see together, what meals they will eat during the week, what TV programs they will watch, etc.

Example of a Meeting

Ms. Black has a junior high school self-contained special education class of 10 students. Four of the students have classic autism, two of the students in the class are nonverbal, and one student is difficult to understand due to language delay.

Ms. Black has arranged a corner of the classroom with a plant, soft light from a lamp she brought from home, and a banner showing the school mascot. When the students come into the classroom, she asks if anyone notices anything different today. Someone points to the corner, and one of the more verbal students says, "What's that for?"

Ms. Black says, "Great question. We now have a special place in our room where we can hold our meetings. From now on, we will have a meeting each Monday afternoon to talk about important things like the good things you do." She holds up a calendar with a picture of the corner placed on each Monday.

Then she says, "Let's go to our special meeting place and practice. You may sit anywhere you want, just get comfortable." When the students have all found a seat, Ms. Black says, "I want to start the meeting by saying something I like about one of you. Then you will say something nice about someone else in this meeting." (*Ms. Black picks a student who is perhaps the least popular or most challenging student in the class.*) She says, "I really like how Billy always comes into class laughing and having a good time."

Now Ms. Black says, "I want you to say something nice about someone. You need to look at that person (*she holds up a visual of looking at someone you are talking to*) and tell them what you like about them. It can be anything, but it must be something nice. The person to whom the nice comment is directed must look at the friend who is talking to her. Who wants to be first?" (*It is important to choose someone who will be successful.*) When the first child has given the compliment, Ms. Black may say, "Thank you, Jason. You did a nice job. I know Karen liked what you said. I also saw that Billy and Emma were watching as you complimented Karen; they listened and kept their hands to themselves." (*At this point Ms. Black takes out a visual showing an icon with the word "listen." She also shows a visual of an icon showing "hands to yourself." A third visual could be an icon of a student talking and a happy face, indicating that something nice was said.*)

Ms. Black now says, "Who wants to be next?" Zack volunteers. Ms. Black knows Zack has very limited expressive language. She says, "Thanks Zack, who do you want to say something nice to?" Zack looks at William, and Ms. Black immediately says, "Great choice! William is a good friend. What do you like about William?" Zack smiles but does not answer her question. Ms. Black says, "William has a really neat shirt on today. Do you like his shirt?" Zack smiles again, and Ms. Black says, "Great, you do like his shirt."

Next, Jimmy gets up from the group and starts walking toward the computer. Ms. Black says, "Jimmy, I think it's time we had a little snack during our meeting. Would you go to the snack cabinet and get the raisins and crackers?" Jimmy looks at her and says, "What?" She tells him to come to her and gives him pictures of the raisins and crackers. Jimmy gets the snacks and brings them back to the group.

At this point, Ms. Black thanks Jimmy and tells everyone that sometimes they will have snacks during the meeting but that everyone must be with the group to share in the snack. She asks Jimmy if he will go to each of the students and let them choose if they want raisins or crackers. Jimmy is encouraged to say each student's name and ask, "_____, Do you want raisins or crackers?" Mary uses her voice output device and says, "Crackers, please." The students get their snack from Jimmy and are told to look at Jimmy and say, "Thanks."

When Jimmy is finished passing out the snacks, Ms. Black says, "Wow, Jimmy, you are a really good server. I think you deserve two extra crackers." She encourages others to tell Jimmy what a good job he did.

After all the children have finished the snack, Ms. Black asks who wants to be next, and the procedure for giving compliments continues. When all the students have had a turn, Ms. Black says, "I have one more compliment to give. I think you are all awesome. You looked at the person you were talking to (*she holds up the visual*). You all said something nice about that person (*she holds up the visual*). You thanked each other (*she holds up the visual*). You kept your hands and feet to yourselves (*she holds up the visual*). You also did an outstanding job with the snacks. I can't wait until our next meeting! Now it is time to check your schedules."

References

Gerberding, J. L. (2007). *Statement on autism spectrum disorders: CDC research and prevention activities: Before the Committee on Appropriations, Subcommittee on Labor, Heath and Human Service, Education and Related Agencies*. US Senate. Retrieved from www.cdc.gov/washington/testimony/2007/t20070417.htm

Myles, B. S., Trautman, M. L., & Schelvan, R. L. (2013). *The hidden curriculum for understanding unstated rules in social situations for adolescents and young adults* (2nd ed.). Shawnee Mission, KS: AAPC Publishing.

Recess Treasure Hunt

Purpose

Recess and other unstructured activities are challenging for most students with autism and related exceptionalities (Machalicek et al., 2009). Many typical students list recess, lunch, and P.E. as their favorite activities of the day; however, students on the autism spectrum often have difficulty during these times, finding the sophisticated social interactions of other students overwhelming. When this is combined with the myriad sensory input the students experience during recess, lunch, and other unstructured times, they often withdraw, act out, become anxious, or just refrain from participating in social activities.

The purpose of this lesson is to help the student with autism experience a positive social interaction by participating in an interesting and motivating activity with another student. The "treasure hunt" is designed to be carried out by pairs of students, who, together, decipher the clues and share in the excitement of searching for and discovering the treasure.

Targeted Skill Categories From the FSSA

Look at the list of skill categories below and determine if any of them pose a need for your students. For example, you may have students who do not know what to do with themselves at recess (Play Skills), often get into trouble with other students (Individual Impulse Control), and seem to have no friends (Understanding of the Concept of Friendship). This might then be a good lesson for these students.

- Ability to Communicate Effectively With Communication Partner
- Individual Impulse Control
- Personal Responsibility
- Play Skills
- Problem-Solving Strategies
- Reads, Interprets, and Responds to Social Cues
- Self-Advocacy Skills
- Transitions
- Understanding of the Concept of Friendship
- Willingness to Do Non-Preferred Things

Recommended Evidence-Based Practices

The following evidence-based practices are recommended for this lesson.

- Choice Making
- Fading
- Friends Teaching Friends
- Joint Action Routines (JARS)
- Modeling
- Picture Exchange Communication System (PECS)
- Pivotal Response Training
- Priming
- Prompting
- Shaping
- Social Narratives
- Social Scripts
- Teaching at the Point of Performance
- Using Special Interests
- Visual Environmental Supports

Considerations for This Lesson

Each student's FSSA and/or IEP do(es) not need to be memorized. However, the instructor should be familiar with the overall possibilities of the treasure hunt and how each student's needs and abilities fit into this activity.

In this lesson, students will be working in teams of two. The main academic skills needed are reading and comprehending written or pictorial directions. If one of the students is not able to perform the skills, pair him/her with a student who is. Each student may be able to do some of the objectives the other student is working on and will have an opportunity to practice some of his/her own goals and objectives as well. These specific objectives may include listening to a friend, offering help, and acting on someone else's ideas or opinions. Students may have the opportunity to generalize their abilities by teaching or modeling.

Materials

The following materials are optional. Materials selection depends on the age, ability, and special interests of the students involved in the treasure hunt.

1. Create written or pictorial instructions or guidelines for the treasure hunt. These may also be read and explained by the teacher and discussed with the students.

2. Select treasures that are motivating for both students and the team. This often includes objects that are part of both students' particular interests or obsessions.

3. Write and/or illustrate clues that lead the students from one playground location to another. Each team will have a set of clues that lead to a specific treasure. This way the instructor has personalized treasures for each student. The clues may be presented in written or pictorial form depending on the abilities of the students. It may be necessary to include aspects of a student's particular interest or obsession in order to keep him or her motivated to continue. This might be a picture or sticker of Thomas the Tank Engine on the clue. The number and complexity of the clues depend on the students' abilities, attention spans, and the time available for this activity.

4. Include one or two "help cards" with the clues so if the students are "stuck," they know they have a way to get help.

5. Develop a list of students who are paired based on their skill levels and personalities. At first the teacher will want to choose the students who are to work together, but later when the students are all familiar with the process, it might be informative to see who the students select as a treasure hunt partner. Some students might choose the person next to them, others may choose their best friend, while yet others might not know how to choose a partner and, therefore, need help. If the teacher foresees that there may be problems with students selecting a teammate themselves, choices may be given for an appropriate partner.

Steps in Implementing This Lesson

Hide the treasure. Have instructions and clues prepared, organized, and ready for the students to use.

1. Introduce the activity and explain that students will be working with a friend to find a hidden treasure. If necessary, describe what a treasure hunt is.

2. Present the treasure hunt instructions, clues, and help cards.

3. As necessary, "walk" the students through their first attempts at completing a treasure hunt. Initially, students may need frequent reinforcement if hesitant to participate. Encourage the students to support and help each other by modeling this behavior and providing cues or prompts when necessary.

4. As the students work together through the clues, compliment them on any appropriate social skills they used.

5. When you think the students are ready, give each team directions for a treasure hunt so they can practice this procedure as independently as possible. Some teams may be able to do a few steps on their own but need help with other parts of the procedure.

6. Observe how the students work together, paying attention to any inappropriate social behaviors that need to be addressed during future lessons. Consider any extensions or challenges you might want to incorporate into the lesson the next time.

Extension Activities for Students Who Are Higher Functioning

- Have students design and plan treasure hunts for each other, another class, teachers, or administrators.

- Incorporate maps, directions, and map keys. Use Google Earth to locate the school playground and use that image as part of the treasure hunt.

- Incorporate a directive into each clue for a specific social skill that the pair of students is to do together before moving on. For example, they may have to give each other a "high five," ask their partner a question (favorite food, what he/she did last night, etc.), or give each other a compliment before they go on to the next treasure hunt location.

Extensions for Parents

Encourage and work with parents to do any or all of the following:

- Do a treasure hunt as a Saturday morning activity in the backyard or at a park. It might be done with siblings or friends.

- As a variation, have siblings develop a treasure hunt for each other.

Example of a Recess Treasure Hunt

Ms. White has a self-contained class of seven students; at least three of them are on the autism spectrum. All of her students need guidance in interacting with other students at recess.

After arriving at school, Ms. White (or her designee) tapes signs "sand box" and "fence" on the sandbox and fence, respectively. She then gives the sign to the teacher who will be on recess duty. This teacher may hold the sign during recess or tape it to her back.

Ms. White explains to two students (whom she has chosen) that they will be working together to try to find a treasure. The students are told that there is something hidden on the playground and that they are to find it. The first clue is given to the students.

Clue #1	
Go to the sandbox	
Dig in the corners	
Find Clue #2 in baggie in the sand	

After the team has found Clue #2 in a plastic baggie, they take it out and read it.

Clue #2	
Go to the fence	
Look at the bottom of the first board	
Find Clue #3 in baggie	

After the team has found Clue #3 in a plastic baggie, they take it out and read it.

Clue #3	
Go to the teacher on the playground	
Ask her nicely for the treasure	

After the team has finished this activity, ask them to bring their clues into the classroom. They now tell everyone about the fun they had and answer questions from the other students.

Reference

Machalicek, W., Shogren, K., Lang, R., Rispoli, M., O'Reilly, M., Franco, J. H., & Sigafoos, J. (2009). Increasing play and decreasing the challenging behavior of children with autism during recess with activity schedules and task correspondent training. *Research in Autism Spectrum Disorders, 3*(2), 547-555.

Cooking Activity

Purpose

Activities involving cooking and eating together are natural opportunities for social interactions (Shepherd, 2009). The social skills used while the students are planning what they will cook are different from the ones that they will use while working in the kitchen together. The social interactions that occur while sitting at a table together and enjoying a delicious meal are different yet. Lessons that take the students through the planning, cooking, and eating of favorite foods are frequently very motivating, and are also a way to teach meaningful vocational and life skills in addition to social interaction skills.

The purpose of this lesson is to encourage students to interact with one another in a variety of ways during a fun and motivating set of activities. The type and difficulty of the foods that are prepared should be tailored to the ages, ability levels, and composition of the groups of students cooking together.

Targeted Skill Categories From the FSSA

Look at the list of skill categories below and determine if any of them pose a need for your students. Some of the students may not be willing to try new foods (Willingness to Do Non-Preferred Things), may be reluctant to ask for more (Self-Advocacy Skills), or may chew with their mouths open (Manners). If so, this is a good lesson for them.

- Ability to Communicate Effectively With Communication Partner
- Environmental Regulation Skills
- Individual Impulse Control
- Personal Responsibility
- Manners
- Problem-Solving Strategies
- Reads, Interprets, and Responds to Social Cues
- Self-Advocacy Skills
- Transitions
- Willingness to Do Non-Preferred Things

Recommended Evidence-Based Practices

The following evidence-based practices are recommended for this lesson.

- Choice Making
- Errorless Learning
- Fading
- Friends Teaching Friends
- Functional Routines (Rules and Routines)
- Joint Action Routines (JARS)
- Modeling
- Picture Exchange Communication System (PECS)
- Pivotal Response Training
- Priming
- Prompting
- Social Narratives
- Social Scripts
- Teaching at the Point of Performance
- Visual Environmental Supports

Considerations for This Lesson

The social skills instructor needs to know each student's social skills objectives as well as the characteristics and personalities of the students that would enable them to work together.

The preparation prior to this lesson will vary based on the students' goals and objectives. When working with students with a range of abilities, each part of the activity (deciding on "rules" for cooking, deciding what to cook, planning who is going to cook together, and grocery shopping) is modified to meet the needs of various students.

This part of the lesson has been written to include detailed steps so that instructors might see the potential social opportunities of the cooking experience. The lesson should be tailored to meet the students' specific social needs and any limitations of the school setting such as having no refrigerator or stove, limited opportunities to go into the community to shop, student food allergies, or special diets.

1. Identify students' social skills objectives that might be addressed in the lesson. Remember that the purpose of the lesson is to teach, encourage, and promote social interactions within the context of the cooking activity.

2. Consider the opportunities and limitations of the school setting and administrative guidelines as they relate to this activity.

3. Determine a realistic timeline for the total activity. Various social skills will be taught during the eating phase of the lesson. It is important to allow enough time to enjoy a relaxed meal during which manners, trying new foods, appropriate table conversation, and many other social skills are addressed.

4. Decide which aspects of the activity the students will get to choose (such as what food to cook) and which ones the instructor will decide.

5. Plan a way to tell the parents about the project. For example, ask the students to talk to their parents about cooking in the classroom, send home a handout about the project, or hold a meeting with the parents to discuss the cooking project.

6. Create a "procedures and rules chart" for cooking in the classroom.

7. Decide on the types of food that the students will cook. This lesson includes recipes for cooked foods as well as non-cooked foods and some excellent picture recipe resources. "Cooking in a Cup" activities provide opportunities for individualization and allow each student to participate in each step of the cooking process. Remember that

Cooking Lesson Prodecures and Rules

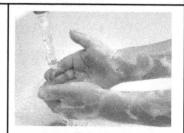

1. **Wash your hands.**	
2. **Use knives and sharp objects carefully.**	
3. **Ask your teacher to help with items that are hot.**	
4. **Keep your hands away from your face.**	
5. **Do your assigned job.**	

the backs of many food boxes such as cake mixes, cookie dough, and macaroni and cheese present recipes in pictorial form.

8. Make a list of ingredients to be obtained and/or purchased.

9. Decide on how the ingredients will be obtained. Will the students have a community-based experience going to the grocery store to purchase the ingredients? Will the teacher bring the ingredients? Will the students bring specific things from home?

10. Plan for all of the related activities and who will be responsible. Some of these tasks include setting the table (perhaps using placemats outlined with flatware, plates, cups, napkins), cleaning the table, washing dishes, putting food away, and sweeping the floor. Remember to set up and teach procedures exactly as they are to be done each time, as many students on the autism spectrum repeat activities the way they did them the first time.

Materials

Materials selection depends mainly on the age and ability levels of the students involved in the cooking activity.

1. Written or pictorial instructions or guidelines for cooking that are read aloud, explained by the teacher, and discussed with the students.

2. Utensils, cooking equipment, food, serving flatware, dishes, and napkins.

3. Equipment for cleaning up after the cooking experience.

4. Recipes, recipe books, and on-line resources

RECIPES

Cooked
English Muffin Pizza
Omelets in a Baggie (gluten-free)
Ultimate Quesadilla Dip (gluten-free) (microwave)
Bubble Pizza
Marble Chocolate Treats
Mall Cookies (gluten-free)

Non-Cooked
Ice Cream in a Baggie (gluten-free)
Trail Mix (substitute Chex® cereal for pretzels and Cheerios® to make gluten-free)
Edible Fun Dough
Pudding in a Cup
Counting Fruit Salad (gluten-free)

ENGLISH MUFFIN PIZZA

INGREDIENTS

English muffins
½ lb. sausage, crumbled
1-2 chicken breasts
pepperoni
mozzarella cheese (shredded)

8 oz. can pizza sauce
½ tsp. oregano
½ tsp. parsley flakes
olive oil
foil

DIRECTIONS

1. Wash hands.

2. Pre-heat oven to 350 degrees.

3. Place foil on cookie sheet.

4. Separate English muffins and place on foil on baking sheet.

5. Brown the sausage.

6. Cut the chicken into pieces about ¼ inch square and brown in olive oil.

7. Place 3 tablespoons of pizza sauce on each English muffin.

8. Sprinkle grated mozzarella cheese on top of pizza sauce on each English muffin.

9. Bake for 3 minutes.

10. Take out of oven and add pepperoni, cooked sausage, cooked chicken, spices or whatever is desired.

11. Add more cheese if desired.

12. Put back into the oven and bake for 4 more minutes.

OMELETS IN A BAGGIE

INGREDIENTS

18 eggs
1 cup milk
1 tsp. salt
½ tsp. pepper
4 cups of shredded cheese
1 cup diced ham
Optional: chopped tomatoes, mushrooms, and green onions

1. Boil 5 cups of water in large pot.

2. Beat eggs, milk, salt, and pepper in electric mixer for about 5 minutes until completely mixed.

3. Dice ham into small squares.

4. Add shredded cheese, diced ham.

5. Pour 1/4 of egg, cheese, and ham mixture into freezer baggie and seal TIGHTLY.

6. Dip baggie of egg, cheese, and ham mixture into hot water and let rest in water until edges of egg, cheese, and ham mixture begin cooking.

7. Remove baggie and tilt until rest of egg mixture is on side of baggie. Put baggie back into the water and cook until all of mixture is an omelet.

4X

8. Repeat 4 times.

9. Serve omelets with chopped tomatoes, mushrooms, or other desired ingredients.

ULTIMATE QUESO DIP

INGREDIENTS

1 lb. round bread loaf
1 lb. (16 oz.) Velveeta® Pasteurized Prepared Cheese Product
1 undrained can (10 oz.) Ro-Tel® diced Tomatoes & Green Chilies

1. Lengthwise cut slice from top of 1 lb. round bread loaf.

2. Remove center of loaf, leaving 1-inch-thick shell.

3. Cut 1 lb. (16 oz.) Velveeta® Pasteurized Prepared Cheese Product into 1/2-inch cubes.

4. Place cheese in medium microwaveable bowl.

5. Stir in 1 undrained can (10 oz.) Ro-Tel® diced Tomatoes & Green Chilies.

6. Microwave on HIGH 5 min. or until Velveeta® is melted and mixture is well blended, stirring after 3 min.

7. Pour into bread shell. Serve with bread squares or chips.

BUBBLE PIZZA

INGREDIENTS

1 can refrigerator biscuits
1 cup pizza sauce
1/2 cup mozzarella cheese
1/2 cup miscellaneous toppings (optional)

1. Cut biscuits into small pieces.

2. Combine in bowl with sauce, 1/4 cup cheese, and toppings if desired.

3. Grease a 9 X13" baking pan. Pour ingredients into pan.

4. Bake at 350 degrees for 25 minutes. Top with remaining 1/4 cheese. Bake another 5 minutes. Enjoy!

MARBLE CHOCOLATE TREATS

INGREDIENTS

8 1/2 Honey Maid Honey Grahams®, broken in half (17 squares)
6 squares Baker's® Semi-Sweet Baking Chocolate
1/2 cup creamy peanut butter
3 squares Baker's Premium White Baking Chocolate®

1. LINE 13 X 9" pan with foil, with ends of foil extending over sides of pan.

2. ARRANGE grahams on bottom of pan, cutting as needed to completely cover bottom of pan: set aside.

3. MICROWAVE: semi-sweet chocolate and peanut butter in medium microwavable bowl on HIGH 1 1/2 – 2 minutes or until chocolate is completely melted, stirring every 30 sec. Stir until well blended.

4. POUR over grahams; spread with spatula to cover completely.

4. REPEAT: microwave melting steps with the white chocolate.

5. DRIP spoonfuls of the white chocolate over chocolate-covered grahams.

6. IMMEDIATELY CUT through the chocolate mixtures with knife several times for tiger-stripe effect.

7. REFRIGERATE at least 1 hour or until firm. Use foil handles to remove dessert from pan. Peel off foil. Cut into bars. Store in tightly covered container in refrigerator.

ICE CREAM IN A BAG

INGREDIENTS

1/2 cup milk
1/4 tsp. vanilla
1 tbsp. sugar
rock salt
ice (lots)

1. Mix milk, vanilla, and sugar together in small bag.

2. Mix salt and ice in larger bag.

3. Place small baggie inside larger baggie.

4. Shake 7-10 minutes until the milk, vanilla, and sugar become ice cream.

5. Open the larger bag and carefully take out the smaller bag of ice cream.

6. Wipe off the smaller bag, open it carefully, and enjoy your ice cream.

EDIBLE FUN DOUGH

INGREDIENTS

1 cup peanut butter
1 cup honey
2 cups powdered milk

1. Measure 1 cup peanut butter.

2. Measure 1 cup honey.

3. Measure 2 cups powdered milk.

4. Mix all ingredients together in a bowl. Add more powdered milk if necessary to make a workable dough.

5. Form the dough into balls and other shapes.

PUDDING

One 3.4 ounce box of instant pudding mix will make 4 individual servings.

INGREDIENTS

1/3 cup milk
2 tablespoons pudding mix

1. Measure 1/3 cup milk.

2. Measure 2 tablespoons pudding mix.

3. Stir ingredients together in a 5-ounce paper cup until firm enough for spoon to stand upright in center of pudding.

COUNTING FRUIT SALAD

INGREDIENTS

 1 can pineapple

2 apples

3 oranges

4 bananas

 5 tbs. sunflower seeds

 6 tsp. raisins

7 tsp. honey

 1. Wash apples.

 2. Put cut-up food in bowl in the order given.

Allow the children to do the adding and counting. A chart to measure would be most appropriate.

TRAIL MIX

INGREDIENTS

3 cups Cheerios®

2 cups pretzel sticks

½ cup raisins

1 cup M&Ms®

¾ cup peanuts

Pour ingredients in a bowl and stir everything together.

RECIPE BOOKS:

Visual Recipes: A Cookbook for Non-Readers by T. Orth (2006)

The Picture Cookbook: No-Cook Recipes for the Special Chef by J. Dassonville & E. McDow (2008)

The Ultimate Step-by-Step Kid's First Cookbook by N. McDougall (2009)

Children's Quick and Easy Cookbook by A. Wilkes (2006)

Kids' First Cookbook: Delicious-Nutritious Treats to Make Yourself! by the American Cancer Society (1999)

Individual Child-Portion Cup Cooking Picture Recipes by B. J. Foote (1993)

Messipes: A Microwave Cookbook of Deliciously Messy Masterpieces by L. Gordon (1996)

Book Cooks: Literature-Based Classroom Cooking by J. Bruno (1991)

Book Cooks: Literature-Based Classroom Cooking by M. Bierele & T. Lynes (1992)

ONLINE RESOURCES:

www.tinsnips.org – This special education resource shares a variety of teaching tools and activities with teachers of students who have autism spectrum disorders and related developmental disabilities. The cooking section is called "What's Cooking" and includes many very clearly illustrated picture recipes.

www.symbolworld.org/learning/cooking/index.htm – This website is created by Widgit software specifically for symbol users. It has materials for all ages and includes a cooking section with easy-to-use recipes of foods many students will want to make and eat, from sandwiches to macaroni and cheese.

www.bry-backmanor.org/picturerecipe6b.html – This website provides all types of materials for students, including holiday icons, worksheets, and other resources. We are particularly interested in the link to picture recipes that include applesauce crunch, gelatin recipes, stone soup, peanut butter snack, and many other foods that might appeal to students on the autism spectrum.

www.kids-cooking-activities.com – This website, started by a mother for her son's kindergarten class, has a wealth of information about cooking with students, from recipes to materials needed to tips for cooking healthy.

Steps in Implementing This Lesson

1. Tell the students about the project. Introduce them to the procedures and rules chart and ask for their input. Be sure to discuss a variety of rules that are important for working in the kitchen.

2. Discuss the theme of the cooking lesson (breakfast foods, snack foods, desserts, etc.). Depending on the students' abilities, ask for recommendations of foods to make, or give them two choices using a visual choice board.

3. With the students, make a list of the ingredients that need to be purchased. The term "making a list" may have different meanings to different students. For some, it may mean matching items on the back of a box to icons that they will affix with Velcro® to a 3 x 5 card. For others, it might mean writing or typing a list. If this is an extension of a previous cooking lesson, some of the ingredients may already be available, such as salt or sugar. Students might measure to make certain they have enough of the ingredient left over for the recipe. Discuss buying only the ingredients and the correct amounts needed for the cooking lesson. For example, some ingredients may spoil if not used right away. It is also important to spend money on only the needed ingredients so that you don't run out of money.

4. Obtain the ingredients. As appropriate, let the students be involved in this step. If possible, go on a community outing to a grocery store and have students use the grocery lists they compiled. This is an important step toward independence. Discuss such things as the location of various food items within the store, where to check out, who is going to pay, and how to ask for help.

5. If appropriate, ask students to choose who they will work with and what they will be responsible for making. For some students, it will be necessary to assign partners and the food they are to make.

6. Plan for all of the tasks involved in food preparation, cooking, serving, and cleanup and who will be responsible for each one.

7. Prepare and cook the food.

8. Enjoy the food together. Model positive statements about the food, manners, and what a good job everyone did. Encourage students to use table manners such as remaining seated until everyone has finished eating, using utensils and napkins appropriately, and politely declining a food offered to them.

9. Get together to discuss what was good or what went well and how to change or improve the activity in the future, at the level appropriate for the students. Model positive comments about the food preparation, taste of the food, and cleanup procedures. Ask the students, and encourage them to ask each other, such questions as, "What was your favorite thing about this activity?," "What was your favorite food we made?," "Will you make it for your family?"

Extension Activities for Students Who Are Higher Functioning

- Invite guests (parents, administrators, other students) to enjoy the food with your students.

- Use ethnic foods recommended by the children and their parents to expand understanding and appreciation of each other.

- Make cookbooks for students that contain recipes they prepared in class. Incorporate digital pictures of the cooking equipment and ingredients used with each recipe. Include photographs of the students enjoying the cooking activities during each step of the process.

- Allow students to look through recipe books and select a recipe they would like to make.

Extensions for Parents

Encourage and work with parents to do any or all of the following:

- Allow your child to teach you how to make some of the foods made in class.

- Remember that students who watch television frequently enjoy watching shows on the Food Network and preparing recipes they learn about at home with their family.

- As a fun activity at home, remove the lid from a covered electric popcorn popper placed on a clean sheet in the middle of the floor. Proceed to make popcorn as usual. As the kernels pop and fly out, family members get to eat the popcorn that comes closest to them. If they get a lot, they are encouraged to share with others who do not have as much.

Adaptations

Many students with autism have sensory problems (Myles et al., 2004), including olfactory (smell) sensitivity. For these students, it might be helpful to start having them in the cooking area during the beginning of the activity when the cooking smells are less noticeable. When they start becoming bothered by the smells, allow them to leave the area if necessary. As their tolerance for food odors increase, let them participate in more phases of the cooking activity.

- Often students with classic autism have difficulty with certain textures (Twachtman-Reilly, Amaral, & Zebrowski, 2008) of food. They may find the feel of certain foods in their mouth to be unpleasant and/or they may be reluctant to touch specific foods with their hands because of the texture. Yogurt, puddings, and Jell-O® are frequently problematic. Mixing a favorite cereal, fruit, or crushed cookies into these foods may help the student try a previously difficult food.

- Some students have a very limited repertoire of foods they are willing to eat (Cermak, Curtin, & Bandani, 2010). Expand this list by using foods or flavors that the student already likes. For example, try offering applesauce or apple pie filling to a student who likes apple juice as a stepping stone to introducing pieces of an apple.

- Keep in mind the types of food your students' families eat. Helping to desensitize a student to a food the family often eats is extremely helpful. In preparation for this, you might ask parents, "If you could get your child to enjoy just one more food, what would it be?"

- Use the Internet or computer software to look up pictures of foods and cooking materials. Use these pictures to transform typical recipes into pictorial recipes.

References and Resources

American Cancer Society. (1999). *Kids' first cookbook: Delicious-nutritious treats to make yourself!* Atlanta, GA: Author.

Bierele, M., & Lynes, T. (1992). *Book cooks: Literature-based classroom cooking*. Cypress, CA: Creative Teaching Press, Inc.

Bruno, J. (1991). *Book cooks: Literature-based classroom cooking*. Cypress, CA: Creative Teaching Press, Inc.

Cermak, S., Curtin, C., & Bandani, L. (2010). Food selectivity and sensory sensitivity in children with autism spectrum disorders. *Journal of the American Dietetic Association, 110*(2), 238-246.

Dassonville, J., & McDow, E. (2008). *The picture cookbook: No-cook recipes for the special chef*. Vancouver, BC: Granville Island Publishing.

Foote, B. J. (1993). *Individual child-portion cup cooking picture recipes*. Ithaca, NY: Early Educators Press.

Gordon, L. (1996). *Messipes: A microwave cookbook of deliciously messy masterpieces*. New York, NY: Random House.

McDougall, N. (2009). *The ultimate step-by-step kid's first cookbook*. Leicester, UK: Anness Publishing, Ltd.

Myles, B. S., Hagiwara, T., Dunn, W., Rinner, L., Reese, M., Huggins, A., & Becker, S. (2004). Sensory issues in children with Asperger Syndrome and autism. *Education and Training in Developmental Disabilities, 39*(4), 283-290.

Orth, T. (2006). *Visual recipes: A cookbook for non-readers.* Shawnee Mission, KS: AAPC Publishing.

Shepherd, T. L. (2009). Teaching dining skills to students with emotional and behavior disorders. *Teaching Exceptional Children Plus, 5*(5). Retrieved from http://escholarship.bc.edu/education/tecplus/vol5/iss5/art2

Twachtman-Reilly, J., Amaral, S. C., & Zebrowski, P. P. (2008). Addressing feeding disorders in children on the autism spectrum in school based settings: Physiological and behavioral Issues. *Language, Speech and Hearing Services in Schools, 39*(2), 261-272.

Wilkes, A. (2006). *Children's quick and easy cookbook.* New York, NY: DK Children.

ONLINE RESOURCES:

(See page 84 for description.)

www.tinsnips.org

www.symbolworld.org/learning/cooking/index.htm

www.bry-backmanor.org/picturerecipe6b.html

www.kids-cooking-activities.com

Activities While Waiting

Purpose

Waiting is one of the greatest challenges for students (Sicile-Kira, 2010). No one likes to wait to eat, to use the computer, or to get on the bus. Students with classic autism often find waiting even more challenging because they have trouble entertaining themselves productively while waiting. They do not socialize while waiting, play pretend games, or compare favorite items or joke with other students. Consequently, periods during the day that involve waiting must be planned well.

The purpose of this lesson is to make waiting time more tolerable for students with classic autism by teaching them things to do that are fun and help them engage with others. The following activities can be replicated in other situations where students must wait.

Targeted Skill Categories From the FSSA

Look at the list of skill categories below and determine if any of them pose a need for your students. For example, one or more of your students may have difficulty accepting redirection (Personal Responsibility), may have a hard time waiting in line (Environmental Regulation Skills), or might not follow the positive examples of others (Problem-Solving Strategies). If so, this lesson would be helpful for these students.

- Ability to Communicate Effectively With Communication Partner
- Environmental Regulation Skills
- Individual Impulse Control
- Manners
- Personal Responsibility
- Play Skills
- Problem-Solving Strategies
- Reads, Interprets, and Responds to Social Cues
- Self-Advocacy Skills
- Transitions
- Willingness to Do Non-Preferred Things

Recommended Evidence-Based Practices

The following evidence-based practices are recommended for this lesson.

- Choice Making
- Fading
- Friends Teaching Friends
- Functional Routines (Rules and Routines)
- Joint Action Routines (JARS)
- Modeling
- Picture Exchange Communication System (PECS)
- Pivotal Response Training
- Priming
- Prompting
- Shaping
- Social Narratives
- Social Scripts
- Teaching at the Point of Performance
- Using Special Interests
- Visual Environmental Supports

Considerations for This Lesson

The social skills instructor must be familiar with each student's social skills needs as well as communication abilities, patterns of behavior, and special interests. When required to wait, a student with classic autism is likely to respond by turning to self-stimulatory activities, delayed echolalia, or acting out as a way of coping with the unpleasant task of waiting.

This lesson suggests using activities and materials that are interesting to the student in order to help him or her change a behavior or develop a new, difficult skill such as waiting. During the beginning stages of the activities, students need more modeling, suggestions, and guidance from the instructor to know what to say and do. When they become familiar with the "games," they will be more self-directed, creative, and participatory.

This lesson applies to any situation in which a student with classic autism must wait. Planning is critical, considering that many of these students are impulsive and impatient and try to avoid situations in which they are not allowed to do what they want to do. This lesson suggests strategies that may be used in a number of situations and settings during the school day.

Many students with classic autism have sensory issues that even further affect their ability to wait. The lights, noise, and/or smells in the environment may be overwhelming and result in problematic behaviors as the students are unable to filter the normal sensory input (Bogdashina, 2003; Grandin, 2000; Myles et al., 2004). It is important to analyze what may be causing these behaviors and help the student by bringing earplugs, avoiding standing under bright lights, or gradually desensitizing her to the input that is causing the discomfort. This involves exposing them to a small amount of the sensory input, and after a short period of time (perhaps 30 seconds) allowing them to leave the area, putting on earphones, or doing whatever acceptable strategies they might have been taught to use to escape the unpleasant input. The exposure time is gradually increased as the student gains ability to tolerate it.

You are encouraged to supplement the games, activities, and recommendations in this lesson with successful classroom strategies with which the students are familiar. For example, many instructors review the lunch menu or upcoming activities with visuals, give choices when possible, and use First/Then boards, meaningful reinforcers, reward charts, social narratives, and other behavioral strategies on a regular basis.

Materials

Few special materials are necessary for this lesson. It is important to have items needed to help students tolerate uncomfortable sensory input and materials needed to implement strategies for helping replace inappropriate behaviors such as visuals and reinforcers. Other materials for individualizing the lesson are suggested, such as response cards for students who are nonverbal when the game calls for a verbal response.

Steps in Implementing This Lesson

Students with classic autism who are very young or demonstrate particularly challenging behaviors should generally not be expected to wait at the cafeteria, the bus, the gym, or other settings within the school until the issues associated with the waiting problems have been addressed. When these students must wait, they should be given their favorite items to hold, jobs such as pushing a wheelchair or cart with supervision, or other productive activities that will help divert their attention and energies.

Things to Do While Waiting

1. "Guess, then count how many ..."

   • boys will walk by while waiting in the hall

   • teachers will be in the cafeteria while waiting for lunch

   • books are on the cart as you are waiting for story time

   • cars will pass before we see the bus while waiting to go home

   Nonverbal students might have a portable choice board with pictures of boys, teachers, books, and cars. They are to select the picture of the item to be counted by the class.

2. "Guess what color ..."

   • the next teacher who walks by our line in the hall will be wearing

   • the teacher on cafeteria duty will be wearing

   • book that the librarian will read to us

   • car will pass next as we wait to go home

   Nonverbal students might have a portable choice board with colored cards attached. They are to "guess what color" by selecting the appropriate card.

3. "Who's the first to see ..."

   • the next teacher who walks by our line in the hall

   • a girl wearing red in the cafeteria

   • a book with a dog on the cover in the library

   • a truck drive by as we wait to go home

   An instructor, paraeducator, or student buddy might be paired with a student who is not able to do this activity independently. The helper reminds the student what to watch for through the use of auditory cues, pictures, or other visual cues. The helper then encourages the student to point when he sees the identified item. The activity should be modified to meet the student's ability level, communication skills, and interests. For example, if the student is not yet able to identify colors, he may be asked to look for the next girl who walks by rather than the next girl wearing red. Or, if the student is very interested in cars, he participates by looking for cars rather than having to look for trucks.

4. "Find the next letter ..."

   Students are to find letters in alphabetical order. If one student finds a sign, poster, name tag, etc., with a word that begins with an "A," the students look for another with a word that begins with a "B," and so forth.

   – while waiting in the hallway

   – while waiting in the cafeteria

   – while waiting in the library

   – while waiting for the bus (license plates, signs, trucks, etc.)

   This activity may be modified for a student who is not able to find the letter in a word without additional supports. Such a student might be given a letter card to match to a sign as the other students find the identified letter.

Extension Activities for Students Who Are Higher Functioning

As the students become familiar with and enjoy the waiting games suggested here, encourage them to make up their own games. This might involve using a special interest of one or more of the students. For example, students might be asked to guess an identified student's favorite toy, color, or food. The instructor might suggest that the students remember what this student picks to eat in the cafeteria, what colors the student wears a lot, or what activities the student picks for free time.

It is very productive to teach students how to wait because as they get older and/or are in situations outside of the school environment, they are often required to wait. It is recommended that the same strategy of giving students interesting things to do during times when they are required to wait be used in other settings and situations.

The FSSA shows that a student may be at differing levels of learning in many of the areas assessed. For example, maybe she has acquired waiting skills through the use of the above activities when waiting for the bus to go home from school each day. But the same student may have trouble waiting for the bus to arrive when being picked up from a CBI (community-based instruction) or job-training site. This would show us that she needs the same objective but at the generalization level of learning so she becomes capable of waiting for a bus in different settings and with different people.

The following situations provide opportunities for generalization of skills acquired at school in different settings and situations outside of the school environment. This helps foster independence and lifelong skills.

- Waiting in line to check out at the grocery store
- Waiting to be served in a restaurant
- Waiting at the doctor's office
- Riding in a car or on an airplane on a family trip
- Waiting in traffic
- Waiting for the movie to start

Extensions for Parents

Encourage and work with parents to do any or all of the following:

- Use the games that have been successful at school when the students have difficulty waiting at home or in the community.
- Tell your child's teacher his/her special waiting games to be used in class while letting everyone know whose game this is.

Example of Activity While Waiting

Mr. Green has a high school class with eight students, four of them have classic autism and have trouble waiting in line in the cafeteria.

Each day before going to the cafeteria, Mr. Green talks to the students about different things the food server may say or be wearing when they see her. He asks Natasha to guess if the server will have on earrings, asks Johnny to guess what she will say to him, and asks Jackie to guess what color blouse she will be wearing. These questions are individualized to meet the students' various communication levels and interests. *(It is helpful to choose an effervescent cafeteria employee who always says or does something, preferably something funny. Be sure to warn the cafeteria employee about the game.)*

Johnny says, "She'll give me a high five." Natasha, who is nonverbal, is given cards of various colors that she can use to tell everyone what color blouse she thinks the server will be wearing. Natasha guesses the server will have on a white blouse today. Jackie is given a picture of earrings, another picture of a necklace, and a picture of a watch. She holds up the picture of the watch because she thinks the server will wear one today.

While waiting in line for their turn to choose their lunch, Mr. Green congratulates Natasha and Jackie for being correct and teases Johnny because the server said, "Hi handsome," before giving him a high five.

To generalize this activity, Mr. Green used it during other times when the students had to wait during the day. For example, he asked the students to guess what the bus driver would say or be wearing when they get on the bus. He asked them to guess what their moms would say or be wearing when they get off the bus.

References

Bogdashina, O. (2003). *Sensory perceptual issues in autism and Asperger's Syndrome: Different sensory experiences, different perceptual worlds.* London, UK: Jessica Kingsley.

Grandin, T. (2000). *Autism spectrum disorders fact sheet: Visual thinking, sensory problems and communication difficulties.* Retrieved from www.autism-help.org

Myles, B. S., Hagiwara, T., Dunn, W., Rinner, L., Reese, M., Huggins, A., & Becker, S. (2004). Sensory issues in children with Asperger Syndrome and autism. *Education and Training in Developmental Disabilities, 39*(4), 283-290.

Sicile-Kira, C. (2010, April 20). *How to teach a child or teen with autism the concept of waiting.* Retrieved from http://www.chantalsicile-kira.com/2010/04/445-how-to-teach-a-child-or-teen-with-autism-the-concept-of-waiting/

Games

Purpose

Many students with classic autism have difficulty participating in group games (Orsmond et al., 2004). This lesson is designed to teach these students to participate in group games that other students their age enjoy. By playing the games, students learn, and practice generalizing, important social skills, including sitting at a table with another person, taking turns, watching what someone else is doing, talking while playing the game, learning the academic content of the game (counting, naming letters, colors, etc.), and gaining skills in an activity that can be shared with peers who are not on the autism spectrum.

The students also learn pragmatic language skills, particularly skills related to speaking differently when playing a game. In game-playing situations, people often joke with others by saying such things as, "I'm going to get you now," or "Man, you killed me!" and other such comments that they would not make in typical conversation. Without receiving instruction in this hidden curriculum item, experiencing the different pragmatic forms, and practicing in a game format, students with classic autism will not be able to participate in an appropriate way in this kind of social experience.

Targeted Skill Categories From the FSSA

Look at the list of skill categories below and determine any areas that pose a need for your students. One or more of the students may have difficulty waiting to take a turn (Play Skills), may show disappointment in an inappropriate way after losing a game (Ability to Communicate Effectively With Communication Partner), or might want to leave the game before it is over (Impulse Control). If so, this lesson would be helpful for them.

- Ability to Communicate Effectively With Communication Partner
- Environmental Regulation Skills
- Individual Impulse Control
- Manners
- Personal Responsibility
- Play Skills
- Problem-Solving Strategies
- Reads, Interprets, and Responds to Social Cues
- Self-Advocacy Skills
- Understanding of the Concept of Friendship
- Willingness to Do Non-Preferred Things

Recommended Evidence-Based Practices

The following evidence-based practices are recommended for this lesson.

- Choice Making
- Errorless Learning
- Fading
- Friends Teaching Friends
- Functional Routines (Rules and Routines)
- Joint Action Routines (JARS)
- Modeling
- Picture Exchange Communication System (PECS)
- Pivotal Response Training
- Power Cards
- Priming
- Prompting
- Self-Monitoring Strategies
- Shaping
- Social Autopsies
- Social Narratives
- Social Scripts
- Teaching at the Point of Performance
- Using Special Interests
- Visual Environmental Supports

Recommended Games and Age Groups

GAME	RECOMMENDED AGE GROUP	COMMENTS
Candy Land®	3-10 years	
Chutes and Ladders®	3-10 years	
Perfection®	3-15 years	Adapt by not using timer
"I'm Thinking of ..."	3-15 years	Make sure the subject of the game is age-appropriate
Memory/Concentration	3 years-adult	Make sure the subject of the game is age-appropriate
Go Fish®	5 years-adult	Make sure the subject of the game is age-appropriate
UNO®	5 years-adult	Make sure the subject of the game is age-appropriate
Monopoly®	5 years-adult	Use Monopoly Junior and/or other Monopoly games that might be of interest (Baseball Monopoly, etc.) as appropriate
Connect Four®	5 years-adult	Adapt for younger students by having them take turns dropping checkers
Dominoes	5 years-adult	Make sure the subject of the game is age-appropriate
LRC (Left, Right, Center)	5 years-adult	Provide assistance for students who don't know left and right
Yahtzee®	5 years-adult	Use Yahtzee Junior when appropriate
Chinese Checkers®	8 years-adult	
Skipbo®	8 years-adult	Number skills are required
20 Questions	8 years-adult	Commercial versions of this game are available
Guess Who?®	8 years-adult	This is excellent for helping build theory-of-mind skills
Guess Where?®	adult	This is excellent for helping build theory-of-mind skills
Trivial Pursuit®	adult	Make sure the subject of the game is age-appropriate

Considerations for This Lesson

The social skills instructor teaching the game must be familiar with the students and their social, communication, and academic abilities. In addition, it is necessary to have an understanding of the purpose of the game for each student or the goals and objectives that are being taught. For some students, the goal is being able to sit in the circle or at the table for the duration of the game. For other students, the objective might be to lose the game in a gracious way and be willing to say something nice to the person who won.

The instructor must also be very familiar with the game and the modifications and adaptations that can and should be made prior to playing with the students. For example,

- When students are nonverbal, such games as *Candy Land* (for younger students) and *UNO* or *Bingo* (for older students) are good because they require limited verbal responses. If students are unable to say, "*Uno!*" or "*Bingo!*," they should be taught to raise their hand to indicate when they have won.

- We want students to interact with each other during the game. This might involve pointing to the student who is next, clapping for another student, or giving the winner a "high five" or "thumbs-up."

- Games might need to be modified greatly for some students. For example, the *UNO* cards might be dealt and each person takes a turn throwing one of his or her cards into a box in the middle of the circle instead of playing *UNO* in the traditional way.

Remember that if modifications and adaptations are made, some students with classic autism will find it difficult to change from the way they first played the game. However, it may be important for these students to transition to playing by the unmodified rules in a protected environment. For example, a paraeducator or teacher may play the game with the student using the standard rules and encourage her to follow these rules. Praise all efforts and successes as well as help the student accept the possible disappointment.

An important part of playing the game is to know how long it should last. It is sometimes helpful to end the game when everyone is having fun and wants to keep playing, even if this is before the actual end of the game. In this way, the students will be more likely to want to play again. Sometimes students don't want to stop playing the game. Use of predetermined ending points such as setting a timer or Time Timer® (www.timetimer.com) telling everyone they have one more turn, or using a natural stopping point such as the bus arriving or lunchtime will be helpful.

Materials

Materials depend on the game being played. Materials selection depends mainly on the age and ability levels of the students involved in the games.

- The game itself.

- A battery-powered card shuffler if the game involves playing cards. This is a way to involve students who can't participate in any other way. It is important to emphasize how important it is to have the cards shuffled and that this student really helped.

- Card holders made from two plastic lids that have been connected with a brad in the middle are often helpful for students who have a difficult time holding cards.

- Visually depicted rules of the game, if necessary.

- Reinforcers, visuals, and other supports to help implement behavior plans and understand game rules.

Steps in Implementing This Lesson

1. Have table, chairs, and materials organized and ready for students.

2. Explain the game, using visual supports as needed. Model how to play with another teacher or a student who is familiar with the game.

3. Explain that the purpose of the game is to have fun. Winning is good, but not as important as having fun.

4. Play the game with the students. Model and encourage them to communicate appropriate things to the other players. It might be helpful for the teacher to play with the student on a one-to-one basis first. Next, play with the student with two teachers (perhaps the teacher and a paraeducator) to practice waiting and sharing. Gradually add players, as appropriate for a given game.

5. At the end of the game, briefly talk to the student about all of the things he did well.

6. Remember or make notes of the things the student did well and the challenges she still has. When planning the goals and objectives for next time, be sure to incorporate these observations. It is sometimes important to stay with one game until the student understands it well and, ideally, enjoys playing it.

Extension Activities for Students Who Are Higher Functioning

- Incorporate students' special interests in the game, if at all possible. For example, in playing 20 Questions, encourage students to choose a topic that incorporates their special interest.

- Have a student who is nonverbal select the next game using a choice board.

- Challenge the students to create a way to play the game so that everyone can participate. For example, with *UNO*, only match colors. Use *Connect Four* as a game to teach turn-taking by dropping the pieces into any available slot at the correct time.

Extensions for Parents

Encourage and work with parents to do any or all of the following:

- Play games together on a regular basis. As the student learns to play a game at school, let the parents know so they can play the same game at home as well.

- Use the adaptations that have been made to the game for your child at school or communicated through newsletters, daily logs sent home, or verbally. Emphasize the social skills that are being taught during the game, such as taking turns, complimenting another player, or being a good loser.

- Start a family tradition of playing a game before bed each Friday and/or Saturday night.

Reference

Orsmond, G. I., Krauss, M. W., & Seltzer, M. M. (2004). Peer relationships and social and recreational activities among adolescents and adults with autism. *Journal of Autism and Developmental Disabilities, 34*(3), 245-256.

The Hidden Curriculum

Purpose

Students with classic autism have difficulty with the unwritten social rules all around us. This area is especially challenging for social skills instructors and parents to address because there is no written curriculum that can be adapted from general education (Garnett, 1984; Hemmings, 2000; Jackson, 1968; Kanpol, 1989; Lavoie, 2005; Myles et al., 2013).

Typical students learn the so-called "hidden curriculum" by watching, listening, and imitating their families, peers, classmates and older students. For example, these students learn what they should and should not say and do to make friends, have others like them, and generally get along socially. They also learn from watching others' experiences and mistakes in social situations (Duke, Nowicki, & Martin, 1996; Garcia-Winner & Crooke, 2009; Lavoie, 2005; Siegel, 2003). An awareness of the nuances of the hidden curriculum is beneficial for all students, as well as for new students coming to the school, exchange students from a different culture, or anyone who could be helped by knowing the unwritten but "special rules" of students in a school.

Students with classic autism do not seem to understand what to say and do or who to watch and imitate in social situations (Weiss & Harris, 2001). These skills must be explicitly taught so that they will be better able to make and keep friends and participate more fully in school and community life.

The purpose of the activities in this lesson is to help the student with classic autism learn and practice the hidden curriculum in a safe and secure environment. For example, Fatina was in the school cafeteria eating her lunch. She finished and was still hungry and the girl next to her had a half-eaten hamburger on her tray. Fatina asked the girl if she could have the hamburger. The girl looked at her in a strange way and said, "I don't think so!" Fatina didn't understand why the girl responded as she did. At home her mother would give her any leftovers if she wanted them. In the classroom, the teacher talked to the class about asking for food from others, what types of food we share (not half-eaten food), and the difference between sharing food with your family and sharing food at school with the person sitting next to you.

> Do not include items that fall into the category of school rules, such as walking in the hallways, as they are not part of the hidden curriculum.

Targeted Skill Categories From the FSSA

Look at the list of skill categories below and determine if any areas pose a need for your students. Do some of your students try to get others' attention in the wrong way (Ability to Communicate Effectively With Communication Partner)? Do your students irritate others because they don't stop when asked to (Reads, Interprets, and Responds to Social Cues)? Does one of your students tease another child in the class (Understanding of the Concept of Friendship)? If so, this lesson will be helpful for them.

- Ability to Communicate Effectively With Communication Partner
- Environmental Regulation Skills
- Individual Impulse Control
- Manners
- Personal Responsibility
- Play Skills
- Problem-Solving Strategies
- Reads, Interprets, and Responds to Social Cues
- Response to Inappropriate Suggestions, Requests and Dares
- Understanding of the Concept of Friendship
- Willingness to Do Non-Preferred Things

Recommended Evidence-Based Practices

The following evidence-based practices are recommended for this lesson.

- Choice Making
- Fading
- Friends Teaching Friends
- Functional Routines (Rules and Routines)
- Modeling
- Pivotal Response Training
- Priming
- Prompting
- Social Autopsies
- Social Narratives
- Shaping
- Teaching at the Point of Performance
- Visual Environmental Supports

Considerations for This Lesson

The needs of students with classic autism related to the hidden curriculum are extremely individualized. As the hidden curriculum is almost infinite in scope and depth, it is important to consider teaching a set of general social rules that can be used to address a variety of challenging social behaviors. For example, teaching students to keep their hands in their pockets or by their sides while walking through stores will cover a variety of individual hidden curriculum student needs, including not touching merchandise, not touching other people, and not taking things that don't belong to them.

If students at different levels are being taught at the same time, it is important to encourage students who have more advanced skills and understanding to help the other students. This provides them with an opportunity to generalize their abilities by teaching or modeling for another student or by using their skills in a new or different situation.

Steps in Implementing This Lesson

Activity One: Hidden Curriculum Shapes Books

Materials Needed:

- Materials for students to make their own hidden curriculum book – poster board, markers, digital pictures, magazines to cut pictures from, pictures from the Internet, scissors, glue, staplers, etc.

- Paper cut-outs in shapes of hidden curriculum topics, such as the shape of a school bus for bus riding topics, the shape of a hamburger for food topics, and the shape of a slide for playground topics.

Steps in Implementing Activity One

1. Decide what hidden curriculum topic to teach and make into a book. The books may be about social rules for greeting others, riding the bus, sharing food, or any other hidden curriculum topic that is causing students social difficulties.

2. Create a paper cut-out in the shape of the hidden curriculum topic.

3. Give everyone the shape and discuss the hidden curriculum items that are appropriate for the setting and the individual needs of the students. Although the general topic will be the same for each student, individual books may contain different hidden curriculum items.

4. Have the students make their own hidden curriculum "books." Help them decorate and put together their books to the extent needed.

5. Practice the skills illustrated in their books.

6. Keep the books in class and discuss them and add to them periodically.

Activity Two: **Hidden Curriculum Calendar**
Materials Needed

- Photographs of the students demonstrating hidden curriculum concepts

- Pictures representing hidden curriculum concepts from magazines, the Internet, etc.

- A large, blank calendar with the squares large enough to accommodate the picture being used to illustrate the hidden curriculum behavior of the week

Steps in Implementing Activity Two

1. Identify specific areas of the school, such as the hallway, cafeteria, playground, bus, etc., in which hidden curriculum pitfalls exist.

2. Select four to five hidden curriculum items that address expected behaviors in the specific setting and work on one per week for a month. For example, if the hallway is selected, the hidden curriculum items could include remaining at arm's distance from the person in front of you in line, stopping when the person in front of you stops, waving back at someone who waves in passing instead of greeting her verbally, remaining in line until arriving at the destination (instead of looking or going into a classroom on the way), and keeping your hands off of other people or items in the hallway.

3. Represent the selected hidden curriculum items in written or pictorial form – take digital photographs of students demonstrating the skill or use relevant pictures from other sources.

4. Introduce the day's selected hidden curriculum item along with a picture or simple written explanation. Attach the picture to the calendar on the appropriate day. You might repeat the same picture on several days as you discuss and review the hidden curriculum item and the students understand and begin to use the suggestions.

5. Discuss the day's item with the students – talk about expected behaviors related to the hidden curriculum item and why they are important (so that you don't step on the heel of the person in front of you, so that you don't disrupt another class, etc.). Perhaps have older or more able students explain the importance and reasons for various hidden curriculum items.

6. Have the students use the hidden curriculum item in the setting for which it was recommended. If needed, use visual supports. This might be a picture to remind the student to thank the cafeteria worker after being served. Point out and compliment each student for remembering and using the hidden curriculum item. Use the students' preferred reinforcers as rewards.

7. Consider inviting specific students from a general education class to participate in circle time using the hidden curriculum calendar items the students made. These students might be ones who have shown an interest in befriending students who

might be in need of a special friend. General education teachers are often aware of who these students are and could recommend them. If your school has a Best Buddy program, students in this program are the logical ones to include. Ask if these students know of other hidden curriculum items for the hallways, cafeteria, playground, bus, etc. If your students have trouble relating to the general education students in circle time, consider getting ideas from general education students for additional hidden curriculum behaviors in school settings.

Extensions for Parents

Encourage and work with parents to do any or all of the following:

- Have older or more able students interview/ask their parents and family members what they think the hidden curriculum is in various situations. This might include the hidden curriculum items specific to Grandma's house or hidden curriculum items specific to their place of worship that are important for children to know.

- Carry out a dinner table ritual related to the hidden curriculum. Everyone says one interesting thing that is a part of the hidden curriculum.

- Have a family meeting before going to an unfamiliar place and talk about the hidden curriculum items in that setting.

- Include students who are nonverbal or are more limited in a dinner table activity involving the hidden curriculum. A sibling or parent might suggest that the student sit at the table in a chair other than his/her "regular chair." When the student hesitates or shows reluctance to sit there, someone says, "Right! You know that's mom's chair. Your chair is over here." Even though the student has not spoken or talked about the hidden curriculum concept of "where we usually sit," he or she understands.

Example of the Hidden Curriculum

Ms. Rodriguez has a class of kindergarten-through-third graders who have classic autism. Almost all of the students ride a bus to and from school each day. As part of Ms. Rodriguez' curriculum, she takes the class on community-based trips on a monthly basis. On these trips she uses booklets the students have made, illustrating hidden curriculum behaviors needed on the bus.

During circle time on the day before their monthly CBI trip, Ms. Rodriguez talked about sitting on the bus. She explained that they should find a seat on the bus, sit down and, if they were the first in a row, scoot over next to the window so there would be room for a friend to sit with them.

In preparation, Ms. Rodriguez had taken pictures of two students: one sitting by the window and one in the process of scooting over next to the window. She also took a picture with the two students sharing a seat. She printed copies of each picture for each student in the class and discussed what was happening in the pictures.

Then she asked them to go to their desks and gave them a blank booklet cut in the shape of a school bus and the pictures they discussed during circle time. Students were asked to glue or staple the pictures in order into the pages of their booklets and were encouraged to decorate each page with crayons and markers in any way they wished. At the end of class, Ms. Rodriguez collected the completed booklets, which were marked with each student's name.

The next day before getting on the bus for their CBI trip, the students were given their booklets. Ms. Rodriguez asked them to look at their pictures and reminded them to get on the bus, find a seat, and, if necessary, scoot to the window and make room for a friend to sit next to them. When they got on the bus, Ms. Rodriguez and the paraeducator made a special point of praising and thanking students for demonstrating the appropriate hidden curriculum behavior.

Each month on the day before the CBI trip, Ms. Rodriguez prepared a lesson and pictures to illustrate a new hidden curriculum behavior for the bus. The class reviewed the previous lessons by talking about the pictures in their school bus books and added the new pictures. This procedure was continued throughout the school year. As a result, the students each had a booklet they could take home that was a history of everything they had learned that year about the hidden curriculum involved in riding the school bus.

References and Resources

Duke, M. P., Nowicki, Jr., S., & Martin, E. (1996). *Teaching your child the language of social success.* Atlanta, GA: Peachtree Publishers, Ltd.

Garcia-Winner, M., & Crooke, P. (2009). *Socially curious and curiously social.* San Jose, CA: Social Thinking Publishing, Inc.

Garnett, K. (1984). Some of the problems children encounter in learning a school's hidden curriculum. *Journal of Reading, Writing and Learning Disabilities International, 1*(1), 5-10.

Hemmings, A. (2000). The hidden curriculum corridor. *High School Journal, 83*(2), 1-10.

Jackson, P. (1968). *Life in classrooms.* New York, NY: Holt, Rinehart, & Winston.

Kanpol, B. (1989). Do we dare teach some truths? An argument for teaching more 'hidden curriculum.' *College Student Journal, 23*, 214-217.

Lavoie, R. (2005). *It's so much work to be your friend: Helping the child with learning disabilities find social success.* New York, NY: Simon & Schuster.

Myles, B. S., Trautman, M. L., & Schelvan, R. L. (2013). *The hidden curriculum for understanding unstated rules in social situations for adolescents and young adults* (2nd ed.). Shawnee Mission, KS: AAPC Publishing.

Myles, H. M., & Kolar, A. (2013). *The hidden curriculum and other everyday challenges for elementary-age children with high-functioning autism.* Shawnee Mission, KS: AAPC Publishing.

Seigel, B. (2003). *Helping children with autism learn: Treatment approaches for parents and professionals.* New York, NY: Oxford University Press.

Weiss, M. J., & Harris, S. L. (2001). *Reaching out, joining in: Teaching social skills to young children with autism.* Bethesda, MD: Woodbine House.

Online Resources

Hidden Curriculum apps. Available at www.itunes.com:

Hidden Curriculum on the Go! for Kids

Hidden Curriculum on the Go! for Older Adolescents and Adults

Transitions

Purpose

Transitions are extremely difficult for students on the autism spectrum (Davis, 1987; Dettmer, Simpson, Myles, & Ganz, 2000; Dooley, Wilczenski, & Torem, 2001; Flannery & Horner, 1994; Flannery, O'Neill, & Horner, 1995; Lansing, 1989; Schreibman, 1988; Schreibman, Whalen, & Stahmer, 2000; Sterling-Turner & Jordan, 2007).

One way to help a student who is having difficulty with transitions is to analyze what part(s) of the transition is/are challenging. Common components include (a) the need to leave the present activity, place, and people, which might be difficult for a student who is enjoying what she is doing at the time; (b) the "journey" from the present location to the next location, which might be problematic or frightening due to loud sounds, bright lights, lots of people or other overwhelming sensory input; and (c) the challenge of arriving at and interacting in the new environment perhaps with new people, materials, and activities. Any part of the transition or any combination of parts may cause distress (Doss & Reichle, 1991; McCord, Thomson, & Iwata, 2001).

Please refer to the chart at the end of this lesson, "Transition Challenges," for an in-depth analysis of specific aspects of transitions that might be problematic for a student with classic autism.

In this lesson, strategies are suggested to help with each of these parts of the transition experience. Gaining flexibility and comfort with transitions will help the student participate more fully in a host of situations and settings. This will also increase the number of opportunities the student has to engage with peers, family members, and others in meaningful ways in social situations.

Targeted Skill Categories From the FSSA

Look at the list of skill categories below and determine if any areas pose a need for your students. Do some of your students have trouble keeping their hands to themselves when walking from one classroom to another (Individual Impulse Control)? Do you have a student who yells, protests, or runs off when it's time to go to the gym (Environmental Regulation Skills)? Does one of your students have trouble going into the cafeteria due to the crowd of students there at the same time (Willingness to Do Non-Preferred Things)? If so, this lesson will be helpful for them.

- Ability to Communicate Effectively With Communication Partner
- Environmental Regulation Skills
- Individual Impulse Control

- Manners
- Personal Responsibility
- Problem-Solving Strategies
- Reads, Interprets, and Responds to Social Cues
- Self-Advocacy Skills
- Transitions
- Willingness to do Non-Preferred Things

Recommended Evidence-Based Practices

The following evidence-based practices are recommended for this lesson.

- Choice Making
- Friends Teaching Friends
- Functional Routines (Rules and Routines)
- Modeling
- Power Cards
- Priming
- Prompting
- Self-Monitoring Strategies
- Social Narratives
- Teaching at the Point of Performance
- Visual Environmental Supports

Considerations for This Lesson

The instructor must be familiar with students' goals and objectives, especially in the areas of behavior, communication, and social skills, as well as with each student's ability to speak, remember what has happened previously, and her patterns of behavior. Instructors should also know people, activities, materials, locations, and reinforcers that are important to each student. For many students, the most problematic part of a transition is the feeling of being rushed. Having a set routine such as leaving class 5 minutes early to avoid crowded hallways and have extra time may help make transitions go more smoothly.

In order to select appropriate strategies to help students tolerate transitions, it is necessary to have an idea of the function of the challenging behavior the student demonstrates during the transition. Several potential explanations for difficulties that might occur at each stage of a transition are listed in the Transition Challenges Chart. The A-B-C Functional Transition Chart on page 117 will assist instructors in analyzing the causes of the difficulties that students experience. Once the possible causes of a behavior are determined, appropriate teaching strategies can be implemented.

Materials Needed

- Transition Challenges Chart
- A-B-C Functional Transition Chart
- Students' preferred reinforcers
- Visual and/or auditory timer
- Visual schedules and/or supports
- Social narratives individualized to the student who has difficulty with change
- Transition items individualized for the student, including schedule card or object, comfort items, or items to be used upon arrival (cup to the cafeteria, favorite ball to gym, special tablet to art class)
- Power Card (Gagnon, 2001) individualized to the student who has difficulty with change

Steps in Implementing This Lesson

Some students don't have obvious difficulties with transitions. However, some may have personal concerns and anxieties when faced with change. As a result, using the recommended teaching strategies is helpful for all of your students.

The following strategies may be used with the many transitions students make throughout the day. They do not involve a specific lesson but can be added to the repertoire of tools teachers use to support students on the autism spectrum. Although the strategies are described in general terms in other places in this program, the following explanations illustrate how they may be used to help students who have specific difficulty with transitions.

1. **Choice Making**

   This procedure helps students have a sense of self-determination and power over what they are required to do. It is also helpful for learning to make good choices throughout life.

   Giving students choices is a successful teaching strategy that may be used in helping a student who has difficulty making transitions. The choices can be used to assist the student through the transition itself or as a reward for having successfully completed a transition. At times, the choice is reinforcing enough to also serve as a reward.

Choices should be limited to two options, both of which the student understands and can do. It is important to adjust the choice when used as a reinforcer to make it appropriate and reasonable, given the demands of the task. For example, it would be reasonable to allow a student who had successfully transitioned to the cafeteria for the first time to choose if he wants to be the first in the class to get his food or to select where he wants to sit at the table. It would not be reasonable to let the same student choose to have a fast-food lunch brought to him or to have three extra desserts from the lunch line as a reward for the successful transition to the cafeteria.

2. Friends Teaching Friends

It is important for students to realize that they can learn from friends and peers. Indeed, sometimes it is easier for them to learn from a friend than from an adult. For example, one 20-year-old student who has classic features of autism likes to hold hands with adults or hold on to their arms when transitioning almost anywhere. Her instructor and many other adults have tried to teach her that she is grown up and that it is not appropriate for her to hold onto adults in such situations.

Recently, this young woman and longtime friends in her class were in a mall. The instructor would not hold her hand or let her hold onto her arm. The student then went to one of the boys in the group and tried to hold his arm. He had heard the instructor tell the girl over and over about adult behavior. He gently told his friend that she could walk with him but not hold his arm. He was teaching her that it was more appropriate in this setting for them to walk next to each other. This helped the student realize that hanging onto someone's arm was not what she should do.

3. Functional Routines (Rules and Routines)

Functional routines are those daily events that happen at specific times and provide continuity for the student. They are often followed without a lot of thought – students engage in the routine through habit.

One functional routine that is helpful during transitions is having the student put materials away in specified places. "Cleaning up" is a cue that something different is going to happen. In fact, many classrooms for young students have a "clean-up" song that signals a transition. Another functional routine is having the student check his individual schedule to see what the next activity of the day is. Some routines take place only when a certain activity is to occur. For example, when transitioning to a new location, it is often helpful for a student to carry a needed item. This task is presented as a natural part of the next setting (e.g., gym, cafeteria, music room) and becomes a part of the transitioning routine. If the student is going to the gym, taking a special ball or jump rope might ease a potentially difficult transition. Have the student focus on what he is carrying, how much help it is to have someone do this, and how much you appreciate this.

4. Modeling

Modeling is a teaching procedure in which one person (teacher, paraeducator, another student, sibling, etc.) performs a task while, in this case, the student on the autism spectrum watches and is subsequently expected to follow the positive example. This might be watching another student get the basketball to go to P.E., watching someone put materials away and get in line, or seeing a friend come in from recess, hang up his sweater, and take a chair to circle time.

One important prerequisite for successful modeling is that the student who is to learn by watching focuses on the other person. One way to help a student focus is to have a routine whereby the teacher asks, "Are you ready?" The student knows that always means he is to immediately put his feet on the floor, hands to his sides or on his desk, and look at the person talking. This is practiced daily. Finally, for modeling to be successful, the student must be interested in what is happening, understand what is happening, and have an opportunity to perform the task or behavior later.

5. Power Cards

A Power Card (Gagnon, 2001) is a device for teaching appropriate social behaviors using the student's special interest, person, or character to show what is expected. If, for example, the student has an older brother whom he looks up to, having a picture of the brother walking through the hallway appropriately will help the younger sibling want to do this, too.

The procedure for using a Power Card is to write a narrative that includes the problematic situation, what the special person or character would do in that situation, and what that person or character encourages the student to do. After the story is reviewed with the student, a small card with a picture of the person or character is developed for the student to carry during the transition as a visual reminder of the story.

For example, Miguel usually runs in the hallways between classes. He is afraid he will be late to his next class and becomes agitated. His teacher knows Miguel admires his older brother who is a senior in the same high school. She writes a story that explains that his brother always walks to class because he knows there will be plenty of time to get there before class starts. She explains to Miguel that he has time and that his brother would be happy if he walked to class. She then develops a small card with Miguel's brother's picture saying, "I walk to class and always get there in time. You can walk to your class and will get there on time. There is enough time to get to class." The teacher reviews the story with Miguel before he goes to his next class and reminds him of the card he carries with his brother's picture and wish for Miguel to walk in the hall.

6. Priming

The purpose of priming is to familiarize the student in a non-threatening and encouraging manner with materials, people, locations, and/or activities before he actually experiences them. It is most effective when it is built into the student's routine.

In terms of transition, a teacher might have a picture, object, or other understood symbol representing the new person, location, material, or activity. This is presented, discussed, and manipulated by the student prior to the transition.

7. Prompting

Prompting is used to increase communication, social behaviors, and skills needed for successful transitions. Teachers using prompting understand the student's level of learning and the need to fade prompts as soon as possible while retaining the skill. Reinforcements given after appropriate behaviors are part of the prompting procedures.

In terms of transition, the students might be verbally reminded to say or wave "good-bye" through prompting. Another example of prompting for transition behaviors includes pointing to the door to remind a student to open and hold the door open for the next person exiting.

8. Self-Monitoring Strategies

Being aware of their emotions is important for students with autism in all situations. *The Incredible 5-Point Scale* (Buron & Curtis, 2012) and stress thermometers are tools to help students understand when they are becoming stressed and how to manage their emotions. By rating themselves on these visual scales, students can learn to identify and label their emotions and designate when they might need a break, additional support, or even alone time.

During transitions, these strategies help students and adults identify the onset of stressful feelings prior to problematic behaviors. Such awareness is important in getting needed supports and thereby managing the transition successfully.

9. Social Narratives

Social narratives can contain short written descriptions of situations, a student's problematic reaction, and a more desired social response. They inform the student of appropriate social behavior.

It is important to personalize the narrative by using the student's name, the exact problem the transition is causing, and a possible solution. Add pictures if visual cues help the student better understand and remember the advice in the story.

10. Teaching at the Point of Performance

Teaching at the point of performance is often used during transitions when students are having difficulty with changes that need to be made. Although instructors should always prepare students for transitions, when new or unforeseen situations come up they have to be handled at that time or "at the point of performance." Errors are treated as teachable moments and are dealt with as they occur in a calm and instructive manner.

11. Visual Environmental Supports

There are many different types of visual supports. One of the most common is a visual schedule. Visual schedules showing that there will be a transition to a new activity, location, or person are very helpful, especially when the student is in the habit of using visuals. It is important to emphasize that whatever is on the schedule is what will happen on a given day. That way the student comes to rely on the schedule to show her what will happen, even though events within the schedule are not always at the same time/location. For example, work jobs might be done before lunch or after lunch. The student can be reassured, however, that whatever her schedule shows today is what will happen – today.

It is also important to build into the system of classroom schedules the use of a change or surprise card. Thus, when there is a sudden and/or unforeseen change such as fire drills, lock-downs, a power outage, the absence of a therapist, etc., the "change card" or "surprise card" is on the schedule to signal an unexpected change in plans. After the change, it is time to get back to the normal routine; it is very important to reestablish use of the usual schedule at this point.

Another type of visual support is a visual timer. Many classrooms have a timer that shows an arc of color representing the amount of time until a targeted event. As the time progresses, less and less of the color is shown. When the color is gone, it is time to transition to a new activity, person, or location. This provides a way of handling the difficult concept of time and increases independence, as the student does not have to ask an adult when a specific event is going to happen.

Transition Challenges Chart

LEAVING (OLD)	TRANSITION (JOURNEY)	ARRIVAL (NEW)
Familiar people	**Concerns about sensory aspects**	**Concerns about sensory aspects**
• family	• too loud	• too loud
• peers	• too hot/cold	• too hot/cold
• educators/therapists/other adults	• too bright/dark	• too bright/dark
	• odors	• odors
Familiar tasks	• frightening possibilities – for example, dogs	• frightening possibilities (any aversions)
• known procedures	• too many people – possibly getting bumped	• too many people
• known expectations	• unexpected tastes	• unexpected tastes
• known task demands	• unexpected texture	• unexpected textures of food
		• unexpected colors of food
Familiar environments	**Concerns about unknown routines**	• unfamiliar peers
• sensory familiarity	• expectations (perhaps unknown)	• unfamiliar educators/therapists/other adults
• familiar location of items	• being unable to do (physically)	
• familiar items/furniture, etc.	• being unable to do routine within time frame (being too slow)	**Unfamiliar tasks**
	• not knowing how to do the routine	• unfamiliar procedures
Familiar reinforcers	• not understanding where I'm going	• unfamiliar expectations
• known rewards	• not understanding route to get there	• unfamiliar task demands
• known procedures – rewards	• not understanding directions given for how to get there	
• known options – rewards	• concerns about having to change routes	**Unfamiliar environments**
		• unfamiliar sensory environment
Familiar routines	**Concerns about unknown people**	• unfamiliar location of items
• known schedule	• unknown people making demands	• unfamiliar items/furniture, etc.
• known openings	• not understanding directions	
• known transition routines	• not getting accustomed to people	**Unfamiliar reinforcers**
• known ending routines		• unfamiliar rewards
• known interaction routines		• unfamiliar procedures – rewards
		• unfamiliar options – rewards
Familiar foods		
• foods of familiar texture		**Unfamiliar routines**
• foods of familiar taste		• unfamiliar schedule
• foods of familiar color		• unfamiliar opening routines
• foods of familiar odor		• unfamiliar transition routines
		• unfamiliar ending routines
		• unfamiliar interaction routines

A-B-C Functional Transition Chart

Time	Transition Event 1. Leaving 2. Journey 3. Arrival	**A**ntecedent (what happened right before the behavior)	**B**ehavior (in measurable and observable terms)	**C**onsequence (what happened right after the behavior)	Possible Causes of Behavior

Note. A copy of the A-B-C Functional Transition Chart may be downloaded by the owner of this book from www.aapcpublishing.net/9106

A-B-C Functional Transition Chart – EXAMPLE

Time	Transition Event 1. Leaving 2. Journey 3. Arrival	**A**ntecedent (what happened right before the behavior)	**B**ehavior (in measurable and observable terms)	**C**onsequence (what happened right after the behavior)	Possible Causes of Behavior
11:30	Leaving	Teacher says, "Check your schedules"	Robbie begins yelling, "no, no, no," cries and bangs side of his head with his fists.	Teacher and para educator go to Robbie to stop the head banging. They tell him he can eat in the classroom	1. Robbie doesn't want to leave classroom 2. Robbie doesn't want to go to cafeteria 3. Robbie doesn't want to be in cafeteria 4. Robbie doesn't like to eat cafeteria food

The teacher will now consider each of the four possible causes of the behavior and try various strategies to determine the specific cause of Robbie's behaviors.

Example of Transitioning From a Familiar to an Unfamiliar Adult

Mrs. Johnson is having a group meeting with the students in the class to discuss an upcoming change. She tells the students she will be gone the next day because she has a doctor's appointment. She assures them that she is not sick and that she will be back in class the following day and that their favorite substitute, Mr. Barnes, will be in class with them while she's gone.

She remembers that the last time he substituted, Mrs. Green, the paraeducator, took pictures of him with the class at recess. She shows them these pictures and asks if anyone remembers Mr. Barnes. Some of the students tell her that he was really nice, he played ball with them, and read a favorite story to them. Mrs. Johnson tells the class that they will have a good time with Mr. Barnes and that she wants to hear all about it when she comes back.

She then asks what the students could do to help Mr. Barnes. Clarence says that he will remind Mr. Barnes that the students need to check their schedules. Louisa remembers that Mr. Barnes needs to take the lunch cards to the cafeteria. Mrs. Johnson reminds Emma, who is nonverbal, that she can smile at Mr. Barnes when he comes into the room and wave goodbye at the end of the day. She concludes by telling the students that she knows they will take good care of Mr. Barnes and that she is so happy that they are helpful and remember all of these things that need to be done.

After this meeting, Mrs. Johnson tells Mrs. Green in private that it is very important to let the students do all they can by themselves. This will be a good opportunity for the students to take responsibility and ownership of the class routine while the teacher is absent. Mrs. Green agrees and tells Mrs. Johnson she'll watch what happens and fill her in with the details when she returns.

Extension Activities for Students Who Are Higher Functioning

Some areas in the school where the students must travel have unique sensory challenges. Some hallways have brighter lights, lots of interesting things on the walls, aromas from the cafeteria; the student might encounter heat/cold from having to go outside; and noises of birds, traffic, or dogs barking.

Have the students who are capable of doing so watch and listen and make a chart of all of the things they might encounter during the journey from the classroom to the next location. If any of these circumstances could cause a problem, list possible solutions on the chart and have the students go over them before leaving the classroom.

Transition Example

GOING THROUGH THE HALLS			
What Might Happen	**Problem**	**What to Do**	**Who Suggested**
Another class wants to go around us	Eric doesn't like anyone being ahead of him	Stop briefly, let the class go, talk to Eric about not always being first	Robert
New artwork with interesting textures has just been hung in the halls	Louisa wants to pick off the cotton balls	Ask Louisa to put her hands behind her back and walk by quickly on other side of the hall	Scott
A bell goes off, and it is loud in the hallways	Annie has a hearing sensitivity and often begins yelling with loud noises	Have Annie bring her earphones whenever she leaves the classroom	Robert

Extensions for Parents

Encourage and work with parents to do any or all of the following:

- Whenever possible, make preparations before problems occur is important. For example, if the child has difficulty getting out of the car at Grandma's house, give her a "present" to take to Grandma, have a schedule of events for Grandma's house, or make sure Grandma has the child's favorite cookies on hand.

- Some students have difficulty going to school or to their class in the mornings. Once in a while, have the student bring the teacher a flower from your garden or something else that is very special. A student might be excited about showing the teacher something she made at home. This helps the student look forward to that first difficult transition of the day.

- Use the A-B-C Functional Transition Chart to document your child's responses to transitions. Be sure to write down as much information as possible, including what specific directives or situations occurred prior to any problematic behavior or anxiety. Remember to include anything that happened in preparation for the transition (*Antecedent*), what the problematic behavior or anxiety looks like during the transition (*Behavior*), and what happened immediately after the behavior or anxiety (*Consequence*).

This information will help determine the reasons for the child's difficulty with transitions and enable you to plan interventions that will get him through these times based on the specific reasons for the behavior or anxiety. For example, if the child throws something at you (*Behavior*) when told to put away a favorite toy (*Antecedent*), it may be that being told *without prior warning* that it's time to put away the favorite toy caused the difficulty with the transition. Therefore, it may be important to alter the antecedent by setting a visual timer to communicate to the child when it will be time to change activities.

Using Books to Discuss Difficult Transitions

The Kissing Hand by A. Penn is a delightful book about a raccoon who misses Mommy while at school. Mommy sends something with her child that will stay with him and help him through difficult times. Use this book either as a resource for parents to get ideas of things they could send with their son or daughter to help with transition problems or read the book to a child and discuss.

Goodbye House by F. Asch is a picture book showing, in simple terms, how a parent helped her child adjust to the change to a new home. The same strategies of taking time to say good-bye to important things in our lives may be used with children experiencing other transition difficulties.

Bread and Jam for Frances by R. Hoban describes the food sensitivity and preferences seen in many students on the autism spectrum. This book may be used as a resource for parents dealing with limited food tolerance by a son or daughter. It is a cute book to read and discuss with a child.

The New Teacher by M. Cohen is an illustrated book about children's fears about getting a new teacher. Rumors spread about the new teacher until the first graders meet her and the students, along with the teacher, decide that they are going to have a good time together. This book would be helpful to read with the child in preparation for a transition to a new teacher.

Franklin and the New Teacher by S. Jennings, C. Gagnon, and S. McIntyre is an illustrated book about Franklin who is upset because Mr. Owl, his teacher, hurt his leg and will be absent. Franklin is especially anxious because he doesn't like changes. When he learns that the new teacher, Ms. Koala, is also nervous, he thinks of a great idea for making the new teacher feel better. Reading this book with the child is a good way to get him or her to think of something nice to do for a substitute teacher and at the same time make an otherwise difficult transition easier.

References

Asch, F. (1986). *Goodbye house.* New York, NY: Simon & Schuster.

Buron, K. D., & Curtis, M. (2012). *The incredible 5-point scale: The significantly improved and expanded second edition.* Shawnee Mission, KS: AAPC Publishing.

Cohen, M. (1972). *The new teacher.* New York, NY: Macmillan Publishing Co.

Davis, D. H. (1987). Issues in the development of a recreational program for autistic individuals with severe cognitive and behavioral disorders. In D. J. Cohen & A. M. Donnelan (Eds.), *Handbook of autism and pervasive developmental disorders* (pp. 371-383). Silver Springs, MD: V. H. Winston & Sons.

Dettmer, S., Simpson, R., Myles, B. S., & Ganz, J. (2000). The use of visual supports to facilitate transitions of students with autism. *Focus on Autism and other Developmental Disabilities, 15*(3), 163-189.

Dooley, P., Wilczenski, F., & Torem, C. (2001). Using an activity schedule to smooth school transitions. *Journal of Positive Behavior Interventions, 3*(1), 57-61.

Doss, L. S., & Reichle, J. (1991). Replacing excess behavior with an initial communicative repertoire. In J. Reichle, J. York, & J. Sigafoos (Eds.), *Implementing augmentative and alternative communication: Strategies for learners with severe disabilities* (pp. 215-237). Baltimore, MD: Paul H. Brookes.

Flannery, K. B., & Horner, R. H. (1994). The relationship between predictability and problem behavior for students with severe disabilities. *Journal of Behavioral Education, 4,* 157-176.

Flannery, K. B., O'Neill, R. E., & Horner, R. H. (1995). Including predictability in functional assessment in individual program development. *Education and Treatment of Children, 18,* 498-509.

Gagnon, E. (2001). *Power Cards: Using special interests to motivate children and youth with Asperger Syndrome and autism.* Shawnee Mission, KS: AAPC Publishing.

Hoban, R. (1992). *Bread and jam for Frances.* New York, NY: Harper Collins.

Jennings, S., Gagnon, C., & McIntyre, S. (2004). *Franklin and the new teacher.* Tonawanda, NY: Kids Can Press.

Lansing, M. D. (1989). Education evaluation. In C. Gillberg (Ed.), *Diagnosis and treatment of autism* (pp. 151-166). New York, NY: Plenum Press.

McCord, B. E., Thomson, R. J., & Iwata, B. A. (2001). Functional analysis and treatment of self-injury associated with transitions. *Journal of Applied Behavior Analysis, 34*(2), 195-210.

Penn, A. (1993). *The kissing hand.* Washington, DC: Child & Family Press.

Schreibman, L. E. (1988). *Autism.* Newburg Park, CA: Sage.

Schreibman, L., Whalen, C., & Stahmer, A. (2000). The use of video priming to reduce disruptive transition behavior in children with autism. *Journal of Positive Behavior Interventions, 2*(1), 3-11.

Sterling-Turner, H., & Jordan, S. (2007). Interventions addressing transition difficulties for individuals with autism. *Journal of Psychology in the School, 44*(7), 681-690.

Doing Something Nice for Others

Purpose

Researchers believe an impairment related to theory of mind may result in various deficits in social skills. Theory of mind refers to the ability to understand that the thoughts, feelings, emotions, beliefs, and intentions of others may not be the same as your own (Baron-Cohen, 1995; Baron-Cohen, Leslie, & Frith, 1985; Hadwin, Baron-Cohen, Howlin, & Hill, 1996; Ozonoff & Miller, 1995; Perner, Frith, Leslie, & Leekam, 1989).

Many students with classic autism have difficulty doing something nice for others. The difficulty, then, in doing something nice for others may be as basic as not knowing what the other person would consider nice. It may also be due to a number of additional factors, including being developmentally young, being uncomfortable reaching out to others, and a lack of instruction in how to do nice things for others.

Through the activities in this lesson, students learn in a step-by-step manner what to do for someone else, how to do something for someone else, and how to respond when that person is grateful and appreciative of these acts.

Targeted Skill Categories From the FSSA

Look at the list of skill categories below and determine if any of them pose a need for your students. Some of your students may not understand when others are in need (Understanding of the Concept of Friendship), may be confused by other people's emotions (Reads, Interprets, and Responds to Social Cues) or may be hesitant to try new activities (Willingness to Do Non-Preferred Things). If so, this is a good lesson for these students.

- Ability to Communicate Effectively With Communication Partner
- Problem-Solving Strategies
- Reads, Interprets, and Responds to Social Cues
- Understanding of the Concept of Friendship
- Willingness to Do Non-Preferred Things

Recommended Evidence-Based Practices

The following evidence-based practices are recommended for this lesson.

- Choice Making
- Fading
- Friends Teaching Friends

- Functional Routines (Rules and Routines)
- Modeling
- Pivotal Response Training
- Priming
- Prompting
- Social Narratives
- Teaching at the Point of Performance
- Using Special Interests
- Visual Environmental Supports

Considerations for This Lesson

Instructors should know their students' social, communication, and academic abilities. It is also important to know the people, activities, and materials that are motivating to each student.

Materials

The materials needed for this lesson depend upon the activity chosen; the age, interests, and ability levels of the students; and how detailed and in-depth the lesson becomes. Recommended materials are incorporated into the activity steps listed in the next sections.

Steps in Implementing This Lesson

Teaching students to do nice things for others might begin with the instructor pointing out in a very specific way the positive and thoughtful things the students are already doing. This is the beginning of what will ideally be a lifelong process of thinking about what other people need and practicing ways to help meet those needs.

The following activities are examples of ways students can learn how to do something nice for others on a daily basis. It is helpful to take pictures of the students as they participate in these activities.

- Make a very special effort to point out – for everyone to hear – the thoughtful things the students are doing throughout the day. For example, "Thank you, Carlos, for lining up the first time I asked. It really helps us get to lunch faster." The more frequently students can be complimented by name, the better.

- Use incidental teaching strategies by, for example, asking for help carrying something "heavy" to the office, taking something to the principal, or running an errand. Such requests allow the student to not only help someone else but to receive praise and thanks in a very natural and appropriate way. It is also a subtle way to communicate that everyone needs help (even the teacher) and that everyone can do something to help (even a student). Again, be sure to thank and praise the students who helped in front of the class.

- At the end of each school day, have students tell one thing they have seen another student do that was helpful or nice. Students who are nonverbal or cannot otherwise do this may enjoy hearing that someone reported something nice that they did. Teachers might model this by saying, "I saw Jason smiling at his teacher today, and I know that made her feel really good."

- Ask each student (secretly) to do something for another student in the class. Talk with the student about what this might be. (*The point is to have each student think about the ways a friend might need help and how she could be of help.*) Make it a type of game by saying, "Don't tell Mary you are going to help her open her milk at lunch today. When you see her raise her hand for help, say, 'I'll help you.' and open her milk." For a less verbal student, helping someone else might mean holding the door open for a friend. Discuss how it felt to help someone and how you felt when someone helped you.

- Arrange for students who have strong dressing skills to help others who are not classroom friends. Perhaps they could visit very young students and help tie shoes after nap time, button coats before recess, or zip jackets before going home at the end of the day. Afterwards, discuss how the students felt when they were helping someone else.

- Prompt students to think of what others do for them and to thank these people. Discuss how the custodians clean the room each day after school and how this makes it nice for everybody. Have the students draw pictures and dictate thank-you notes to the custodians.

- Arrange for students to participate in school-wide food drives by packing donated items into bags and boxes for delivery to aid agencies.

- Discuss the importance of helping not only individual people but the larger school community and even the environment. Begin a class project of cleaning up the school grounds on a regular basis. Students can pick up items and sort trash from recyclable materials.

- Make a class book with the students that captures their experiences in helping others. Take pictures of the students helping younger students tie their shoes or zip their jackets, perhaps one student holding the door for a friend, another student taking a note to the principal, and a group of students picking up trash from the school yard. Compile these pictures into the book and, as appropriate, have students dictate the sentences that match each picture. Be sure to use their names in these sentences. Perhaps the students could take turns taking the book home to "read" and explain to their families.

Extensions for Parents

Encourage and work with parents to do any or all of the following:

- Talk to your children about how they can help another family member. Teachers may want to share the positive things that happened in this lesson when it was done at school.

- Collect things from every member of the family that would be helpful for another family and take them to the Goodwill or some other agency that is collecting donations.

- Encourage your son or daughter to participate in community drives to donate items for people who have experienced great losses. This might be through your place of worship, local TV station, grocery store, etc.

References

Baron-Cohen, S. (1995). *Mind blindness: An essay on autism and theory of mind.* Cambridge, MA: MIT Press.

Baron-Cohen, S., Leslie, A. M., & Frith, U. (1985). Does the autistic child have a theory of mind? *Cognition, 21*(21), 37-46.

Hadwin, J., Baron-Cohen, S., Howlin, P., & Hill, K. (1996). Can we teach children with autism to understand emotions, belief, or pretense? *Development and Psychopathology, 8,* 345-365.

Ozonoff, S., & Miller, J. (1995). Teaching theory of mind: A new approach to social skills training for individuals with autism. *Journal of Autism and Developmental Disorders, 25,* 415-434.

Perner, J., Frith, U., Leslie, A. M., & Leekam, S. (1989). Exploration of the autistic child's theory of mind: Knowledge, belief, & communication. *Child Development, 60*(3), 689-700.

Show and Tell

Purpose

Demonstrating an intense interest in a specific topic or item is one of the hallmark characteristics of individuals with autism spectrum disorders (American Psychiatric Association, 2000; Turner, 1999). Research has shown that individuals with classic autism are more likely to participate in social interactions when they are allowed or encouraged to talk about or show others an item or topic of special interest to them (Baker, 2000; Baker, Koegel, & Koegel, 1998; Gagnon, 2001). In addition, many students find it comforting to carry objects of special interest with them, and, as a result, may be more willing to engage in difficult or stressful activities such as socializing with others.

The purpose of this lesson is to help students experience positive social interactions by participating in activities that are interesting and motivating. Incorporating items or topics of extreme interest into activities designed to encourage social interactions is an effective way of increasing a student's willingness to participate and decreasing anxiety. The show-and-tell activities in this lesson not only create opportunities to share, but also teach the students how to listen to others.

Targeted Skill Categories From the FSSA

Look at the list of skill categories below and determine if any of them pose a need for your students. For example, you may have students who never participate in group activities because they don't share information when asked (Ability to Communicate Effectively With Communication Partner), find it difficult to wait their turn in a group activity (Individual Impulse Control) and/or have difficulty sharing a preferred activity (Play Skills). If so, this is a good lesson for them.

- Ability to Communicate Effectively With Communication Partner
- Individual Impulse Control
- Personal Responsibility
- Play Skills
- Reads, Interprets, and Responds to Social Cues
- Self-Advocacy Skills
- Transitions
- Understanding of the Concept of Friendship
- Willingness to Do Non-Preferred Things

Recommended Evidence-Based Practices

The following evidence-based practices are recommended for this lesson.
- Choice Making
- Fading
- Friends Teaching Friends
- Functional Routines (Rules and Routines)
- Joint Action Routines (JARS)
- Modeling
- Picture Exchange Communication System (PECS)
- Pivotal Response Training
- Priming
- Prompting
- Shaping
- Social Narratives
- Social Scripts
- Teaching at the Point of Performance
- Using Special Interests
- Visual Environmental Supports

Considerations for This Lesson

This lesson uses a group format and provides an opportunity for students to practice such skills as listening without interrupting, controlling impulses, communicating expressively, and making positive statements to others. Students may have the opportunity to generalize their abilities by "teaching" the group about their item of interest or modeling appropriate listening behavior.

Instructors may wish to prepare a set of "Show and Tell Rules" that encompass such behaviors as looking at and listening to the speaker, taking turns to talk, saying nice things about another student's "show and tell," and asking permission before touching things that belong to others. It is important to take students' cognitive levels and communication skills into consideration when deciding upon the wording of the rules. Present the rules in a visual/pictorial as well as verbal format.

Instructors working with students with verbal abilities may also wish to set a time limit that each student must adhere to prior to sharing their topic or item. Use a visual and/or auditory timer to communicate when the time limit has been reached.

To keep the pace and flow of the lesson moving, consider the students' communication abilities, attention spans, tolerance for waiting, activity level, and distractibility. These characteristics will determine the adaptations and modifications needed for some students and which students are able to participate in this lesson more actively.

Materials

- Show and Tell Rules
- Visual and/or auditory timer
- Student-selected items of interest
- Interesting stim toys – whirl, light up, etc.
- Thematic objects for Secret Sack activity
- Choice board/PECS (Picture Exchange Communication System) book/voice output device, if needed

Steps in Implementing This Lesson

It is important that every student participate in each activity. This sometimes necessitates providing supports and using other partial participation techniques such as giving verbal prompts to the student with limited expressive skills or encouraging the use of voice output devices. For students who are more verbal but have difficulty staying on topic, social scripts or prompting by suggesting the first part of an appropriate response may be helpful.

Activity 1.
Have students bring their favorite "stim" object or an object representing their favorite topic to show and tell. Students take turns "showing and telling" about their objects. Instructors and students ask yes/no questions about the item and the student sharing the object answers their questions with a nod or shake of the head, by pointing, using PECS, or otherwise communicating a response.

Activity 2.
Give students an object that is interesting or exciting (lights up, spins, etc.) but is not their favorite object. Encourage the students to look at, perhaps activate and show others the object, as well as answer simple questions about the object in whatever manner they are able.

Activity 3.
Select a variety of appealing objects that are part of a larger theme, for example, a season, holiday, color of the week, letter of the week, foods from a recently read book (e.g., *The Very Hungry Caterpillar*), and put them in a cloth bag. Ask each student to take a turn removing one item from the bag and showing it to the rest of the group. Encourage students to use whatever forms of expressive communication they typically employ – whether PECS, voice output device, verbal language, signs, or choice board – to state, "I see a ____" or "I have a ____." Students who are able can add descriptors like shape or color to further elaborate on the Secret Sack item they selected.

Activity 4.

Select a topic such as favorite videos, favorite characters, or what the student ate for breakfast and take turns sharing and answering questions about it. Consider, and have available, the types of augmentative communication methods necessary for students to participate as independently as possible. This might require voice output devices, pictures, or choice boards.

Extension Activities for Students Who Are Higher Functioning

- Create a brief questionnaire for students to fill out about themselves. It might include questions about their family, favorite color, activity, food, and/or movie. Students complete the questionnaire by writing, using pictures, or typing their answers on the computer. Then they bring their paper to the group to share. Reading their descriptions may give confidence to students who are hesitant to speak in front of others. As a variation of this activity, have students who are able interview one another and share with the rest of the group what they learned about their friend.

- Have students share their thoughts and experiences or answer questions about an interesting teacher-selected topic.

- Ask students to take turns sharing about a favorite person by saying one thing that is nice about how the person looks or something the person likes. Once students become skilled at commenting on a physical trait or interest of some-one in the group, have them begin working toward sharing something about a group member's personality. Such comments may include why they are a good friend or what they like best about the person.

- To build self-esteem, ask students to share things that they could not do when they were young but now can do well. For example, it might be that they could not use a computer, but now they can. Perhaps they could not write their name but now can do this easily, or they could not tie their shoes but now they help others do this.

- Have students interview someone in the class (perhaps even the instructor or other adult) by asking a short series of questions such as, "What is your favorite animal?," "What is your favorite food?," or "What is your favorite TV program?" The student who did the interview then shares a few things about the person, while others in the group try to guess who was interviewed.

- Have students invite parents, a friend from another class, teachers, or administrators to show and tell. Guests share their favorite items or topics while the students listen, ask questions, and make comments.

- Read aloud (adult or students, as appropriate) books on sharing. Endless possibilities for discussion topics exist, including the following.

   Everybody Cooks Rice by N. Dooley is about a child who visits neighbors' homes at dinnertime and finds that everyone in the neighborhood is having rice, but they cook it in different ways depending on what country they are from. This is a delightful book about not only what we eat that is different but some of the things we have in common. The book also includes a list of recipes for cooking rice that might be used in the classroom.

   What Mary Jo Shared by J. Udry is a book about a kindergarten student who wants to share but each day finds that the other children have better things to share than she does. Her brother helps her, but even so other students always have something better than Mary Jo. One day she brings a special surprise, her father, and shares what he did as a child and telling them that he is now a teacher. Everyone is excited, and Mary Jo is very happy and proud.

   Show and Tell by R. Munsch is a playful book about a boy who brings his baby sister to school in his backpack for show and tell. Students will enjoy the comic situations in which the teacher and other adults find themselves as they try to calm the crying infant. Afterwards, the students all bring their own silly and special show-and-tell items to share with the class.

   Listen and Learn by C. Meiners is one in a series of books that encourage young children to learn and use social skills. In this book, a boy tells his peers about what it means to listen and why it is important to listen. He gives specific examples of listening behaviors that they might use in school and at home, including keeping quiet, watching the person who is talking, thinking about what is being said, and asking questions when he doesn't understand. The book includes a special section for teachers or other adults on ways to reinforce these skills, discussion questions, and games to play after reading the book.

 ## Extensions for Parents

Encourage and work with parents to do any or all of the following:
- Initiate a show-and-tell session for family members and close friends at gift-giving times (birthdays and holidays) that everyone can participate in, either through the use of an augmentative communication device or verbal language.

References

American Psychiatric Association. (2000). *Diagnostic and statistical manual of mental disorders* (DSM-IV-TR, 4th ed.). Washington, DC: Author.

Baker, M. J. (2000). Incorporating the thematic ritualistic behaviors of children with autism into games: Increasing social play interactions with siblings. *The Journal of Positive Behavior Interventions, 2*(2), 66-84.

Baker, M., Koegel, R. L., & Koegel, L. K. (1998). Increasing the social behavior of young children with autism using their obsessive behavior. *The Journal of the Association for Persons with Severe Handicaps, 23*(1), 300-308.

Carle, E. (1969). *The very hungry caterpillar.* New York, NY: Philomel Books.

Dooley, N. (1991). *Everybody cooks rice.* Minneapolis, MN: Millbrook Press.

Gagnon, E. (2001). *Power cards: Using special interests to motivate children and youth with Asperger Syndrome and autism.* Shawnee Mission, KS: AAPC Publishing.

Meiners, C. (2003). *Listen and learn.* Minneapolis, MN: Free Spirit Publishing Inc.

Munsch, R. (1991). *Show and tell.* Buffalo, NY: Annick Press Ltd.

Turner, M. (1999). Annotations: Repetitive behavior in autism: A review of psychological research. *Journal of Child Psychology and Psychiatry, 40*(6), 839-849.

Udry, J. (1966). *What Mary Jo shared.* New York, NY: Scholastic.

Bullying

A Note From the Authors

- Bullying is long-term torment that does not occur between social equals (Pappas, 2012).

- Research on bullying suggests that while many factors can put someone at risk of being a target, bullies tend to choose victims they know their classmates won't defend (Veenstra, Lindenberg, Munniksma, & Dijkstra, 2010).

The topic of bullying is appropriately receiving large amounts of attention in school systems, the media, scholarly research, and in family discussions. The characteristics of classic autism, such as (a) difficulty with theory of mind, (b) problems in communication, and (c) an impaired ability to read facial expressions and body language and predict the intention of others, have been discussed in previous lessons. In light of these characteristics, teaching students with autism to identify bullying, respond to it appropriately, and avoid being bullied is a huge challenge.

The authors of this program have for many years worked with students with classic autism and continue on a daily basis to meet with, observe, and study these individuals. For all of these reasons, this lesson on bullying culminates in the teaching of six behaviors that have been identified as preventive measures to bullying. These behaviors are being taught as rules. There is always a danger in identifying rules such as these as they sometimes might not apply and they might seem to contradict goals of student independence, self-advocacy, and social communication. However, we feel that in matters such as bullying, it is wise to err on the side of being overly conservative or cautious. If students can be more independent than this lesson suggests, please use your professional judgment to encourage and enable them to do so.

Purpose

Many students on the autism spectrum are bullied (Gray, 2000, 2001; Heinrichs, 2003; Humphrey & Symes, 2012; Lavoie, 2005; Montes & Halterman, 2007; van Roekel, Scholte, & Didden, 2010). Inclusive education programming is increasing. This is appropriate, but at the same time, it exposes students with special needs, in particular, autism, to the possibility of more bullying.

Some students do not realize they are being bullied and might respond in inappropriate ways, such as staying around, arguing with the bullies, or having a meltdown. Sometimes students with classic autism even believe the bullies are their friends because they are talking to them. Therefore, it is important to teach strategies to help them identify bullying, avoid being the object of bullying, handle any bullying that is taking place, and prevent bullying from happening in the future. Understanding the concept of bullying also helps students know what real friends do and how they behave.

Having a plan for handling bullying is part of training students with classic autism to achieve greater independence. Bullying can present safety issues that must be addressed. In addition, being able to handle bullying gives students a better self-concept and more self-confidence, and is an important aspect of self-advocacy.

The focus of this lesson is on helping students with classic autism who have limited cognitive and social skills use positive strategies when confronted by any form of bullying. Most of these students are not alone in school or community environments. Being with a caregiver, peer buddy, paraeducator, or other helper precludes others from bullying students who might otherwise be the object of bullying. If, however, students do find themselves in a bullying situation, they must recognize that they need help and have strategies for obtaining such help.

Some students with classic autism may be perceived as bullies themselves because of their size and the behaviors they demonstrate when they are upset, which can frighten others. Due to the students' limited level of understanding, these actions should be addressed in Behavior Intervention Plans, and replacement behaviors must be taught. For example, some students with classic autism may run up to another student and get too close when they want to communicate or see what is happening. This might be perceived as threatening and, if done repeatedly to the same student, might be perceived as bullying. Students with autism should be taught to walk, keep an appropriate distance from the person they want to be with, and communicate their intent through the use of a social script or other practiced phrases.

Targeted Skill Categories From the FSSA

Look at the list of skill categories below and determine if any of them pose a need for your students. For example, you may have students who are not able to determine which appropriate behaviors to imitate (Problem-Solving Strategies), who have difficulty determining what a real friend would and would not do (Understanding of the Concept of Friendship), or are unable to tell the appropriate people when they are hurt (Self-Advocacy). If so, this is a good lesson for them.

- Ability to Communicate Effectively With Communication Partner
- Individual Impulse Control
- Problem-Solving Strategies

- Reads, Interprets, and Responds to Social Cues
- Response to Inappropriate Suggestions, Requests, Dares
- Self-Advocacy Skills
- Understanding of the Concept of Friendship

 ## Recommended Evidence-Based Practices

The following evidence-based practices are recommended for this lesson.

- Choice Making
- Errorless Learning
- Fading
- Pivotal Response Training
- Power Cards
- Priming
- Prompting
- Self-Monitoring Strategies
- Shaping
- Social Autopsies
- Social Narratives
- Social Scripts
- Teaching at the Point of Performance
- Visual Environmental Supports

Many programs that teach about bullying use modeling, role-play, and other simulation activities. While this might be effective for students who are not on the autism spectrum, such strategies are not recommended in this lesson because many students with classic autism have difficulty differentiating real from pretend situations. They think in very concrete terms, and if something is presented as wrong but a teacher or another student does it, even in role-playing, it is difficult for these students to understand that the teacher was just pretending. Conversely, they may not realize a situation is real when they are encountering bullying and may think that they are still pretending.

Another complicating issue is that if a person the student knows bullies her during a simulation, the student may feel that anyone she knows can't be a bully. Or conversely, might think that person is really bullying her. Such misunderstanding is extremely problematic.

Considerations for This Lesson

Bullying is a universal problem in schools. Specifically, up to 46% of adolescents with autism spectrum disorders have experienced bullying (van Roekel et al., 2010). If this is happening in your school, talking with administrators, counselors, teachers, and students about the problem is important.

Neurotypical students who know students in special education classes by name and as individuals usually do not bully or tolerate bullying of these students. Having a buddy program, peer-tutoring program, cross-age tutoring, and/or reverse inclusion program where general education students work and socialize with other students in a special education setting are all ways to build a group of students who advocate for those in special classes (Koegel & LaZebnik, 2012). These programs are of benefit to all students, including students in general education classes.

Instructors must be aware of patterns in the school such as who the potential bullies are, locations where bullying tends to occur, and times when students on the autism spectrum might be especially vulnerable to bullies. It is also necessary for staff to be familiar with the school-wide plan regarding bullying and ensure that the strategies taught to students on the autism spectrum are compatible with and support the school plan.

Materials

- Picture cards:
  - Bullying situations
  - Situations where bullying is NOT happening
  - What to do when you are the object of bullying
  - What NOT to do when you are the object of bullying

- Individualized social narratives

- Individualized Power Cards

Steps in Implementing This Lesson

This lesson is organized into three sections: "What Does Bullying Look Like?," "What to Do in Bullying Situations," and "How to Avoid a Bullying Situation From Happening to Me." The first two sections begin with an informal visual assessment to determine if the student needs to be taught that section or already understands and has mastered the content. If a student does not meet the criterion for mastery, begin teaching that section. However, if the student meets criterion, she is not taught the section. This is to prevent students from getting bored by being retaught information they already know. It also allows the teacher to focus on the students who need and don't understand the content of this section.

When students meet the criteria on both assessments, they are ready to begin working on the third section of this lesson. Instructors may wish to consider having students who are ready for the third section serve as peer tutors for students who are being taught the first two sections. The rationale for teaching all students Section 3, "How to Avoid a Bullying Situation From Happening to Me," is not only the importance of teaching them to stay "out of the line of fire," but to give them proactive behaviors that can be practiced. The authors believe that every student with classic autism can benefit from instruction and practice in implementing the rules taught in this section.

Conduct a brief discussion to prepare students for the lesson. Explain that they are going to learn about bullying. Bullying is not good and may make people feel unhappy, sad, angry, or mad. Let students know that everyone needs to learn about how to take care of themselves because some students may do things to others over and over that are unkind and hurtful – this is called bullying. If this happens, the student being bullied needs to know what to do to take care of himself and be able to execute it.

Section #1: What Does Bullying Look Like?

Informal Assessment

1. Explain to the students that the first thing they need to know about bullying is what it looks like and what it does not look like.

2. Demonstrate the assessment procedure by showing how to sort the pictures on the previous page into groups indicating bullying vs. not bullying. During the demonstration, make sure to talk about the fact that bullying is wrong, bad, hurtful, and unacceptable. If needed, label the stacks with a picture of a red light to indicate where to place the bullying pictures and a picture of a green light to indicate where to place the non-bullying pictures, or whatever other signs/symbols representing "correct" and "incorrect" the student is accustomed to using.

3. Show a student a picture and ask her to place it in the correct pile. Continue with all of the pictures given in this assessment.

4. Students who correctly identify 9 out of the 10 pictures presented in this assessment may go on to the next assessment. Students who don't meet the criterion for this assessment are taught this section.

Teaching Procedures

1. Use the picture cards to define bullying by showing the students what a bully might do. Bullies might hit, push, pinch, trip, and/or laugh at you. They might call you bad names or take things from you. Bullies might also ask you to do things that you don't want to do. In addition, there may be other kids who laugh at you when a bully is doing mean things.

2. For students who demonstrate aggressive behaviors, it is important to explain that being hit, pushed, pinched, tripped, etc., after they have provoked someone else is NOT an act of bullying. Tell these students that it is never OK to hurt another person.

3. After introducing the idea of bullying, reinforce the concept by taking the students on a tour of the school and pointing out any posters, signs, or slogans that are posted as part of the school-wide anti-bullying program.

4. If appropriate, invite students who are not on the autism spectrum (perhaps students from reverse inclusion or buddy programs) to talk about and reiterate simple points about what bullying looks like. Consider suggesting to these general education students that they can serve as powerful advocates for the students on the autism spectrum if they see them confronted by bullying by letting the bully know that they do not approve of their behavior toward the student.

Section #2: What to Do in Bullying Situations

Informal Assessment

1. Conduct a brief discussion to prepare students for this assessment. Tell the students that since they already know what bullying looks like, it is time to learn what to do or what not to do if they are bullied.

2. Demonstrate the assessment procedure by showing how to sort the pictures (see page 137) into groups indicating what to do and what not to do if bullied. If needed, label the stacks with a picture of a green light to indicate where to place the pictures of what to do if bullied and a picture of a red light to indicate where to place the pictures of what not to do if bullied, or whatever other signs/symbols representing "correct" and "incorrect" that the student is accustomed to using.

3. Show a student a picture and ask him to place it in the correct pile. Continue with all of the pictures given in this assessment.

4. Students who correctly identify 9 of the 10 pictures presented in this assessment may go on to section 3, "How to Keep a Bullying Situation From Happening to Me." Students who don't meet this criterion are taught Section 2.

Teaching Procedures

1. Teach students basic strategies for handling bullying situations. These should focus on the importance of staying with another person whenever possible. If students find themselves alone, they should yell, "No!," "Don't do that!," "Stop!," or "Quit!" when approached by someone threatening. They should then walk away from the area as quickly as possible and tell an adult. Emphasize that the student should not stay with the bully or do what the bully tells him to do.

2. Using an individualized social narrative at this point might be helpful. Talk about and read the narrative any time the students go into a possible bullying situation such as waiting at the bus stop, recess, walking in the hallway, P.E., etc.

3. Create individualized Power Cards (Gagnon, 2001) (see examples below) to help remind the students of these strategies. Perhaps have the students participate by suggesting who or what should be on the Power Cards.

(Student's name)	(Student's name)	(Student's name)
Thomas says, "You do not have to do **bad** things other kids tell you to do!"	President Obama says, "You do not have to give your lunch away to another student if you do not want to."	Barney says, "Other students should not take your favorite things. Walk away fast and tell an adult."

Section #3: How to Prevent a Bullying Situation From Happening to Me

There is no assessment for this section. All students are taught Section 3. The information in this section is based on rules that are essential for students with classic autism to know and use.

Teaching Procedures

The main strategy for preventing bullying is to be with someone. Teach the students that whenever they can, they should go places with a friend, another student, a paraeducator, or an adult. Encourage the students to ask another student if they can walk to a class, the cafeteria, and/or the bus with them. Remind them that if the other student says, "No," the appropriate response is to say, "Okay," and walk away. *Always teach students on the spectrum what to say and do so they won't be embarrassed or respond inappropriately.*

Teach students to:

1. **Walk quickly when alone.** Tell the students that the rule is "whenever you are alone in the hallways, you must walk quickly and go directly to where you are going." Watch the students as they practice this rule. Discuss the positive things the students did and remind them if there are things they should do differently.

2. **Stay with a familiar person whenever possible.** Teach the students to remain next to the person with whom they started walking. Tell them to not stop at a locker unless the person they are with stops with them. They are not to walk ahead of their companion or go another route. For students needing more help, pairing them with a responsible student or perhaps an adult is best.

3. **Ask a friend to go along.** Talk with the students about whom they might ask to walk with them in the hallway or when they are going some place alone in the school. For nonverbal students, use a choice board with other students' pictures. In this way the students are discussing friends, and the instructor can monitor if they are making appropriate choices.

4. **Walk directly to where you are going using the route you have been taught.** The essence of this rule is for the student not to go places in the school that might be dangerous. Since this is often difficult for students with classic autism to determine, it is best to teach them how to get to their destination and to always use this route.

5. **Walk quickly past someone who has bullied you in the past. Do not look at them or say anything to them.** Since the students already know what bullying is, talk about staying away from bullies by walking quickly past them. It may be that this person just happens to be in the hallway and has no intention of repeating the bullying. This is a difficult judgment for a student with classic autism to make, so it is important to provide a rule for the situation.

6. **Walk around groups of people, as opposed to walking through crowds or groups.** Some students with classic autism tend to walk through groups of people because it is the shortest way to get to their destination. This sets them up to be at least the object of ridicule, if not a target for bullying. To avoid this possibility, teach the students to walk around any group of people.

Extension Activities for Students Who Are Higher Functioning

- Read and discuss one or more of the following books with the students.

    Move Over Twerp by Martha Alexander is about a boy who is bullied on the bus. He talks with everyone, getting suggestions about what to do. The final pages show his amusing solution to the bullying problem.

    Stop Picking on Me (A First Look At Series) by Pat Thomas is a picture book that teaches about bullying in simple terms. It explores the fears, worries, and questions surrounding bullying. It is based on the belief that the students must first understand what bullying is before they can respond appropriately.

    Rosie's Story by Martine Gogoll is a book about a little girl who is made fun of because of her red hair and freckles. Rosie learns that she is not alone.

    King of the Playground by Phyllis Reynolds Naylor is a book in which Sammy does not let Kevin play on the swings, slide, or monkey bars. After talking to his father, Kevin understands how to respond to Sammy without fighting.

    Amelia Takes Command by Marissa Moss is about Amelia, who is beginning fifth grade, and is being bullied by someone in her class. At Space Camp, she finds the confidence to stand up to the bully at home.

    Bully on the Bus by Carl W. Bosch is a "choose-your-own-ending" book. Students decide what to do when confronted by a bully. Their choices are to ignore, to talk to an adult, to confront the bully, to fight or to reconcile. This is a great culminating activity for this lesson.-

    Oliver Onion – The Onion Who Learns to Accept and Be Himself by Diane Murrell is about Oliver the Onion, who doesn't like himself. But when he decides to try on the "look" of a tempting-looking orange, he soon realizes that he cannot run away from who he is, but should instead celebrate his uniqueness.

- Help students create social autopsies (Lavoie, cited in Bieber, 1994) of situations in which they have experienced bullying. Social autopsies involve discussions, drawings, cartoons of inappropriate social interactions, how someone was hurt by the interaction, and what could be done differently the next time that would be more appropriate. Invent a scenario that the students understand and relate to in order to practice analyzing a bullying situation.

SOCIAL AUTOPSY FOR BULLYING

Cathy and her teacher completed this chart when Cathy returned to class upset after lunch one day

INCIDENT: Cathy was going to the cafeteria and saw a girl who had smiled at her in the hallway for the first time that morning. Now Cathy thought the girl was her good friend. Cathy said, "Hi, can I eat with you today?" The girl, who was with a group of her friends said, "Okay, if you give me your dessert first." Everyone in the group laughed and some of the girls tried to take Cathy's lunch. Cathy ran to the lunchroom crying as the girls continued laughing.
1. IDENTIFY THE ERROR • Cathy stopped to talk to someone she didn't know who was with a group of friends • Cathy asked to eat with the girl when she didn't know her
2. DETERMINE WHO WAS HURT: Cathy was hurt by the girls trying to get her dessert and laughing at her.
3. DETERMINE HOW TO CORRECT THE ERROR: • Cathy should tell her teacher what happened. • Cathy needs to remember that someone smiling once does not mean they are your friend. • Cathy should remember not to stop in the hallways to talk to one girl who is in a group of friends.
4. DEVELOP A PLAN SO THAT THE ERROR DOES NOT OCCUR AGAIN: Review the rules of going through the halls and talking to people you don't know: A. Be with someone else B. Don't stop and talk to people you don't know C. Avoid going to locations through crowds of students D. Stay with friends you know and who you know like you

Extensions for Parents

Encourage and work with parents to do any or all of the following:

• Read the article "Ten Actions ALL Parents Can Take to Help Eliminate Bullying," which describes important, yet practical ideas you can use to make your children more aware of bullying and to create environments at school and at home that are respectful of others' differences. It and other excellent resources for parents regarding bullying may found on the Education.com website.

• Another helpful resource is *Bullying and Students with Disabilities: Summary Report of Parent Focus Group* (2004, May) by Leslie F. Hergert. www.cga.ct.gov/COC/PDFs/bullying/102107_bullying_disabilities.pdf

• The Department of Health and Human Services offers online antibullying courses and information at www.pathwayscourses.samhsa.gov.

References

Alexander, M. (1982). *Move over twerp.* New York, NY: The Dial Press.

Bosch, C. W. (1988). *Bully on the bus.* Seattle, WA: Parenting Press.

Gogoll, M. (1994). *Rosie's story.* New York, NY: Mondo Publishing.

Gray, C. (2000). Gray's guide to bullying part 1: The basics. *The Morning News, 12*(4).

Gray, C. (2001). Gray's guide to bullying part II: The basics. *The Morning News, 13*(1).

Humphrey, N., & Symes, W. (2012). Responses to bullying and use of social support among pupils with autism spectrum disorders (ASDs) in mainstream schools: A qualitative study. *Journal of Research in Special Education Needs, 10*(2), 82-90.

Koegel, L. K., & LaZebnik, C. (2012). *How to stop bullying of kids on the autism spectrum.* Retrieved from www.education.com

Lavoie, R. (2005). *It's so much work to be your friend: Helping the child with learning disabilities find social success.* New York, NY: Simon and Schuster.

Montes, G., & Halterman, J. (2007). Bullying among children with autism and the influence of co-morbidity with ADHD: A population based study. *Ambulatory Pediatrics, 7*(3), 253-257.

Moss, M. (1998). *Amelia takes command.* Middleton, WI: Pleasant Company Publications.

Murrell, D. (2004). *Oliver Onion.* Shawnee Mission, KS: AAPC Publishing.

Naylor, P. R. (1994). *King of the playground.* New York, NY: Simon & Schuster Children's Publishing.

Pappas, S. (2012, March 27). *Bullies target kids with autism, survey finds.* Retrieved from www.livescience.com

Thomas, P. (2000). *Stop picking on me (A first look at series).* Hauppauge, NY: Barron's Educational Series.

van Roekel, E., Scholte, R., & Didden, R. (2010). Bullying among adolescents with autism spectrum disorders: Prevalence and perceptions. *Journal of Autism and Developmental Disorders, 40*(1), 63-73.

Veenstra, R., Lindenberg, A., Munniksma, A., & Dijkstra, J. (2010). The complex relation between bullying, victimization, acceptance and rejection: Giving special attention to status, affection and sex differences. *Child Development, 81*(2), 480-486.

References and Resources

References

Alberto, P. A., & Troutman, A. G. (2008). *Applied behavior analysis for teachers* (8ᵗʰ ed.). Columbus, OH: Merrill Prentice Hall.

Alexander, M. (1982). *Move over twerp.* New York, NY: The Dial Press.

American Cancer Society. (1999). *Kids' first cookbook: Delicious-nutritious treats to make yourself!* Atlanta, GA: American Cancer Society.

American Psychiatric Association. (2000). *Diagnostic and statistical manual of mental disorders* (DSM-IV-TR, 4th ed.). Washington, DC: Author.

Asch, F. (1986). *Goodbye house.* New York, NY: Simon & Schuster.

Baker, M. J. (2000). Incorporating the thematic ritualistic behaviors of children with autism into games: Increasing social play interactions with siblings. *Journal of Positive Behavior Interventions, 2*(2), 66-84.

Baker, M., Koegel, R. L., & Koegel, L. K. (1998). Increasing the social behavior of young children with autism using their obsessive behavior. *Journal of the Association for Persons with Severe Handicaps, 23*(1), 300-308.

Barkley, R. (2000). *Taking charge of ADHD.* New York, NY: Guilford Press.

Baron-Cohen, S. (1995). *Mind blindness: An essay on autism and theory of mind.* Cambridge, MA: MIT Press.

Baron-Cohen, S., Leslie, A. M., & Frith, U. (1985). Does the autistic child have a theory of mind? *Cognition, 21*(21), 37-46.

Bieber, J. (1994). *Learning disabilities and social skills with Richard Lavoie: Last one picked ... first one picked on.* Washington, DC: Public Broadcasting Service.

Bierele, M., & Lynes, T. (1992). *Book cooks: Literature-based classroom cooking.* Cypress, CA: Creative Teaching Press, Inc.

Bogdashina, O. (2003). *Sensory perceptual issues in autism and Asperger's Syndrome: Different sensory experiences, different perceptual worlds.* London, UK: Jessica Kingsley.

Bondy, A., & Frost, L. (2002). *A picture's worth: PECS and other visual communication strategies in autism (Topics in Autism).* Bethesda, MD: Woodbine House.

Bosch, C. W. (1988). *Bully on the bus.* Seattle, WA: Parenting Press.

Brooks, R., & Goldstein, S. (2012). *Raising resilient children with autism spectrum disorders: Strategies for helping them maximize their strengths, cope with adversity, and develop a social mindset.* New York, NY: McGraw Hill.

Bruno, J. (1991). *Book cooks: Literature-based classroom cooking.* Cypress, CA: Creative Teaching Press, Inc.

Buron, K. D., & Curtis, M. (2012). *The incredible 5-point scale: The significantly improved and expanded second edition.* Shawnee Mission, KS: AAPC Publishing.

Carle, E. (1969). *The very hungry caterpillar.* New York, NY: Philomel Books.

Carr, E. G., & Darcy, M. (1990). Setting generality of peer modeling in children with autism. *Journal of Autism and Developmental Disorders, 20*(1), 45-59.

Carter, C. M. (2001). Using choice with game play to increase language skills and interactive behaviors in children with autism. *Journal of Positive Behavioral Intervention, 3*(3), 131-151.

Cermak, S., Curtin, C., & Bandani, L. (2010). Food selectivity and sensory sensitivity in children with autism spectrum disorders. *Journal of the American Dietetic Association, 110*(2), 238-246.

Cohen, M. (1972). *The new teacher.* New York, NY: Macmillan Publishing Co.

Dassonville, J., & McDow, E. (2008). *The picture cookbook: No-cook recipes for the special chef.* Vancouver, BC: Granville Island Publishing.

Davis, D. H. (1987). Issues in the development of a recreational program for autistic individuals with severe cognitive and behavioral disorders. In D. J. Cohen & A. M. Donnelan (Eds.), *Handbook of autism and pervasive developmental disorders* (pp. 371-383). Silver Springs, MD: V. H. Winston & Sons.

Davis, K. M., Boon, R. T., Cihak, D. F., & Fore III, C. (2010). Power cards to improve conversational skills in adolescents with Asperger syndrome. *Focus on Autism and other Developmental Disabilities, 25*(1), 12-22.

Dettmer, S., Simpson, R., Myles, B. S., & Ganz, J. (2000). The use of visual supports to facilitate transitions of students with autism. *Focus on Autism and other Developmental Disabilities, 15*(3), 163-189.

Dooley, N. (1991). *Everybody cooks rice.* Minneapolis, MN: Millbrook Press.

Dooley, P., Wilczenski, F., & Torem, C. (2001). Using an activity schedule to smooth school transitions. *Journal of Positive Behavior Interventions, 3*(1), 57-61.

Doss, L. S., & Reichle, J. (1991). Replacing excess behavior with an initial communicative repertoire. In J. Reichle, J. York, & J. Sigafoos (Eds.), *Implementing augmentative and alternative communication: Strategies for learners with severe disabilities* (pp. 215-237). Baltimore, MD: Paul H. Brookes.

Duke, M. P., Nowicki, Jr., S., & Martin, E. (1996). *Teaching your child the language of social success.* Atlanta, GA: Peachtree Publishers, Ltd.

Duncan, A., & Klinger, L. (2010). Autism spectrum disorders: Building social skills in group, school and community settings. *Social Work with Groups: A Journal of Community and Clinical Practice, 33*(2-3), 175-193.

Dunn, M. A. (2006). *S.O.S.: Social skills in our schools.* Shawnee Mission, KS: AAPC Publishing.

Flannery, K. B., & Horner, R. H. (1994). The relationship between predictability and problem behavior for students with severe disabilities. *Journal of Behavioral Education, 4,* 157-176.

Flannery, K. B., O'Neill, R. E., & Horner, R. H. (1995). Including predictability in functional assessment in individual program development. *Education and Treatment of Children, 18,* 498-509.

Foote, B. J. (1993). *Individual child-portion cup cooking picture recipes.* Ithaca, NY: Early Educators Press.

Gagnon, E. (2001). *Power Cards: Using special interests to motivate children and youth with Asperger Syndrome and autism.* Shawnee Mission, KS: AAPC Publishing.

Garcia-Winner, M., & Crooke, P. (2009). *Socially curious and curiously social.* San Jose, CA: Social Thinking Publishing, Inc.

Garnett, K. (1984). Some of the problems children encounter in learning a school's hidden curriculum. *Journal of Reading, Writing and Learning Disabilities International, 1*(1), 5-10.

Gerberding, J. L. (2007). *Statement on autism spectrum disorders: CDC research and prevention activities: Before the Committee on Appropriations, Subcommittee on Labor, Heath and Human Service, Education and Related Agencies.* U.S. Senate. www.cdc.gov/washington/testimony/2007/t20070417.htm

Gogoll, M. (1994). *Rosie's story.* New York, NY: Mondo Publishing.

Gordon, L. (1996). *Messipes: A microwave cookbook of deliciously messy masterpieces.* New York, NY: Random House.

Grandin, T. (2000). *Autism spectrum disorders fact sheet: Visual thinking, sensory problems and communication difficulties.* Retrieved from www.autism-help.org

Grandin, T. (2008). *The way I see it: A personal look at autism & Asperger's.* Arlington, TX: Future Horizons.

Gray, C. (2000). Gray's guide to bullying part 1: The basics. *The Morning News, 12*(4), 1-24.

Gray, C. (2000). *The new social story book.* Arlington, TX: Future Horizons Inc.

Gray, C. (2001). Gray's guide to bullying part II: The basics. *The Morning News, 13*(1), 1-38.

Hadwin, J., Baron-Cohen, S., Howlin, P., & Hill, K. (1996). Can we teach children with autism to understand emotions, belief, or pretense? *Development and Psychopathology, 8*, 345-365.

Heinrichs, R. (2003). *Perfect targets: Asperger Syndrome and bullying – Practical solutions for surviving the social world.* Overland Park, KS: AAPC Publishing.

Hemmings, A. (2000). The hidden curriculum corridor. *High School Journal, 83*(2), 1-10.

Henry, S., & Myles, B. S. (2013). *The comprehensive autism planning system (CAPS) for individuals with autism spectrum disorders and related disabilities: Integrating best practices throughout the student's day, second edition.* Shawnee Mission, KS: AAPC Publishing.

Hoban, R. (1992). *Bread and jam for Frances.* New York, NY: Harper Collins.

Humphrey, N., & Symes, W. (2012). Responses to bullying and use of social support among pupils with autism spectrum disorders (ASDs) in mainstream schools: A qualitative study. *Journal of Research in Special Education Needs, 10*(2), 82-90.

Jackson, P. (1968). *Life in classrooms.* New York, NY: Holt, Rinehart, & Winston.

Jennings, S., Gagnon, C., & McIntyre, S. (2004). *Franklin and the new teacher.* Tonawanda, NY: Kids Can Press.

Johnston, S., Nelson, C., Evans, J., & Palazolo, K. (2003). The use of visual supports in teaching young children with autism spectrum disorder to initiate interaction. *Augmentative and Alternative Communication, 19*, 86-103.

Kanpol, B. (1989). Do we dare teach some truths? An argument for teaching more 'hidden curriculum.' *College Student Journal, 23*, 214-217.

Kluth, P., & Schwarz, P. (2008). *"Just give him the whale!" 20 ways to use fascinations, areas of expertise, and strengths to support students with autism.* Baltimore, MD: Paul H. Brookes Publishing Company.

Koegel, L. (2012). *Pivotal response treatments: Improving socialization in individuals with autism.* Santa Barbara, CA: Behavior Management Student Organization.

Koegel, R., & Frea, W. (1993). Treatment of social behavior in autism through the modification of pivotal social skills. *Journal of Applied Behavior Analysis, 26,* 369-377.

Koegel, L. K., & LaZebnik, C. (2012). *How to stop bullying of kids on the autism spectrum.* Retrieved from www.education.com

Koegel, R. L., Werner, G. A., Vismara, L. A., & Koegel, L. K. (2005). The effectiveness of contextually supported play-based interactions between children with autism and typically developing peers. *Research and Practice for Persons with Severe Disabilities, 30*(2), 93-102.

Krantz, P. J., & McClannahan, L. (1993). Teaching children with autism to initiate to peers: Effects of a script-fading procedure. *Journal of Applied Behavior Analysis, 26,* 121-132.

Krantz, P. J., & McClannahan, L. (1998). Social interaction skills for children with autism: A script fading procedure for beginning readers. *Journal of Applied Behavior Analysis, 31*(2), 191-202.

Krasny, L., Williams, B. J., Provencal, S., & Ozonoff, S. (2003). Social skills intervention for the autism spectrum: Essential ingredients in a model curriculum. *Child and Adolescent Psychiatric Clinics of North America, 12*(1), 107-122.

Lansing, M. D. (1989). Education evaluation. In C. Gillberg (Ed.), *Diagnosis and treatment of autism* (pp. 151-166). New York, NY: Plenum Press.

Lavoie, R. (2005). *It's so much work to be your friend: Helping the child with learning disabilities find social success.* New York, NY: Simon & Schuster.

Machalicek, W., Shogren, K., Lang, R., Rispoli, M., O'Reilly, M., Franco, J. H., & Sigafoos, J. (2009). Increasing play and decreasing the challenging behavior of children with autism during recess with activity schedules and task correspondent training. *Research in Autism Spectrum Disorders, 3*(2), 547-555.

McClannahan, L. E., & Krantz, P. J. (1999). *Activity schedules for children with autism: Teaching independent behavior.* Bethesda, MD: Woodbine House.

McCord, B. E., Thomson, R. J., & Iwata, B. A. (2001). Functional analysis and treatment of self-injury associated with transitions. *Journal of Applied Behavior Analysis, 34*(2), 195-210.

McDougall, N. (2009). *The ultimate step-by-step kid's first cookbook.* Leicester, UK: Anness Publishing, Ltd.

Meiners, C. (2003). *Listen and learn.* Minneapolis, MN: Free Spirit Publishing Inc.

Mesibov, G. B. (1998). Editorial. *Journal of Autism and Developmental Disorders, 28*(6), 465-466.

Mesibov, G. B., Shea, V., & Schopler, E. (2005). *The TEACCH approach to autism spectrum disorders.* New York, NY: Plenum Press.

Montes, G., & Halterman, J. (2007). Bullying among children with autism and the influence of co-morbidity with ADHD: A population based study. *Ambulatory Pediatrics, 7*(3), 253-257.

Moss, M. (1998). *Amelia takes command.* Middleton, WI: Pleasant Company Publications.

Munsch, R. (1991). *Show and tell.* Buffalo, NY: Annick Press Ltd.

Murrell, D. (2004). *Oliver Onion.* Shawnee Mission, KS: AAPC Publishing.

Myles, B. S., Hagiwara, T., Dunn, W., Rinner, L., Reese, M., Huggins, A., & Becker, S. (2004). Sensory issues in children with Asperger Syndrome and autism. *Education and Training in Developmental Disabilities, 39*(4), 283-290.

Myles, B. S., & Simpson, R. L. (2003). *Asperger Syndrome: A guide for educators and parents* (2nd ed.). Austin, TX: Pro-Ed.

Myles, B. S., Trautman, M. L., & Schelvan, R. L. (2013). *The hidden curriculum for understanding unstated rules in social situations for adolescents and young adults.* Shawnee Mission, KS: AAPC Publishing.

Myles, H. M., & Kolar, A. (2013). *The hidden curriculum and other everyday challenges for elementary-age children with high-functioning autism.* Shawnee Mission, KS: AAPC Publishing.

Naylor, P. R. (1994). *King of the playground.* New York, NY: Simon & Schuster Children's Publishing.

Orsmond, G. I., Krauss, M. W., & Seltzer, M. M. (2004). Peer relationships and social and recreational activities among adolescents and adults with autism. *Journal of Autism and Developmental Disabilities, 34*(3), 245-256.

Orth, T. (2006). *Visual recipes: A cookbook for non-readers.* Shawnee Mission, KS: AAPC Publishing.

Ozonoff, S., & Miller, J. (1995). Teaching theory of mind: A new approach to social skills training for individuals with autism. *Journal of Autism and Developmental Disorders, 25,* 415-434.

Pappas, S. (2012, March 27). *Bullies target kids with autism, survey finds.* Retrieved from www.livescience.com

Penn, A. (1993). *The kissing hand.* Washington, DC: Child & Family Press.

Perner, J., Frith, U., Leslie, A. M., & Leekam, S. (1989). Exploration of the autistic child's theory of mind: Knowledge, belief, & communication. *Child Development, 60*(3), 689-700.

Polirstok, S. R., Dana, L., Buno, S. D., Mongelli, V. D., & Trubia, G. D. (2003). Improving functional communication skills in adolescents and young adults with severe autism using gentle teaching and positive approaches. *Topics in Language Disorders, 23*(2), 146-153.

Rogers, S. J. (2000). Interventions that facilitate socialization in children with autism. *Journal of Autism and Developmental Disorders, 30*(5), 399-409.

Rubin, K. H. (2002). *The friendship factor.* New York, NY: Viking Penguin.

Savner, J. L., & Myles, B. S. (2000). *Making visual supports work in the home and community.* Shawnee Mission, KS: AAPC Publishing.

Sawyer, L., Luiselli, J., Ricciardi, J., & Gower, J. (2005). Teaching a child with autism to share among peers in an integrated pre-school classroom: Acquisition, maintenance and social validation. *Education and Treatment of Children, 28,* 1-10.

Schopler, E., & Mesibov, G. B. (Eds.). (1986). *Social behavior in autism.* New York, NY: Plenum.

Schreibman, L. E. (1988). *Autism.* Newburg Park, CA: Sage.

Schreibman, L., Whalen, C., & Stahmer, A. (2000). The use of video priming to reduce disruptive transition behavior in children with autism. *Journal of Positive Behavior Interventions, 2*(1), 3-11.

Shepherd, T. L. (2009). Teaching dining skills to students with emotional and behavior disorders. *Teaching Exceptional Children Plus, 5*(5). Retrieved from http://escholarship.bc.edu/education/tecplus/vol5/iss5/art2

Sheridan, S. J., & Bahme, D. E. (2003). *Developing social skills groups: Social skills in natural environments.* Houston, TX: Authors.

Sicile-Kira, C. (2010, April 20). *How to teach a child or teen with autism the concept of waiting.* Retrieved from http://www.chantalsicile-kira.com/2010/04/445-how-to-teach-a-child-or-teen-with-autism-the-concept-of-waiting

Siegel, B. (2003). *Helping children with autism learn: Treatment approaches for parents and professionals.* New York, NY: Oxford University Press.

Snyder-McLean, L., Solomonson, B., McLean, J., & Sack, S. (1984). Structuring joint action routines: A strategy for facilitating communication and language development in the classroom. *Seminars in Speech and Language, 5*, 213-228.

Sterling-Turner, H., & Jordan, S. (2007). Interventions addressing transition difficulties for individuals with autism. *Journal of Psychology in the School, 44*(7), 681-690.

Stevenson, C. L., Krantz, T. J., & McClannahan, L. E. (2000). Social interaction skills for children with autism: A script fading procedure for non-readers. *Behavioral Intervention, 15*, 1-20.

Thomas, P. (2000). *Stop picking on me (A first look at series).* Hauppauge, NY: Barron's Educational Series.

Tincani, M., & Devis, K. (2011). Quantitative synthesis and component analysis of single-participant studies on the picture exchange communication system. *Remedial & Special Education, 32*(6), 458-470.

Turner, M. (1999). Annotations: Repetitive behavior in autism: A review of psychological research. *Journal of Child Psychology and Psychiatry, 40*(6), 839-849.

Twachtman-Reilly, J., Amaral, S. C., & Zebrowski, P. P. (2008) Addressing feeding disorders in children on the autism spectrum in school based settings: Physiological and behavioral Issues. *Language, Speech and Hearing Services in Schools, 39*(2), 261-272.

Udry, J. (1966). *What Mary Jo shared.* New York, NY: Scholastic.

van Roekel, E., Scholte, R., & Didden, R., (2010). Bullying among adolescents with autism spectrum disorders: Prevalence and perceptions. *Journal of Autism and Developmental Disorders, 40*(1), 63-73.

Veenstra, R., Lindenberg, A., Munniksma, A., & Dijkstra, J. (2010). The complex relation between bullying, victimization, acceptance and rejection: Giving special attention to status, affection and sex differences. *Child Development, 81*(2), 480-486.

Weiss, M. J., & Harris, S. L. (2001). *Reaching out, joining in: Teaching social skills to young children with autism.* Bethesda, MD: Woodbine House.

Wichnick, A. M., Vener, S. M., Keating, C., & Poulson, C. L. (2009). The effect of a script fading procedure on unscripted social initiations and novel utterances of young children with autism. *Research in Autism Spectrum Disorders, 4*, 51-64.

Zanolli, K., Daggett, J., & Adams, T. (1996). Teaching preschool age autistic children to make spontaneous initiations to peers using priming. *Journal of Autism and Developmental Disorders, 26*(4), 407-422.

Recommended Resources

Arick, J. R., Loos, L., Falco, R., & Krug, D. A. (2004). *The STAR program: Strategies for teaching based on autism research.* Austin, TX: PRO-ED Inc.

Aspy, R., & Grossman, B. (2007). *Underlying characteristics checklists manual: UCC-HF and UCC-CL.* Shawnee Mission, KS: AAPC Publishing.

Aspy, R., & Grossman, B. G. (2011). *The Ziggurat model: A framework for designing comprehensive interventions for high-functioning individuals with autism spectrum disorders, updated and expanded edition.* Shawnee Mission, KS: AAPC Publishing.

Baker, J. (2001). *The social skills picture book: Teaching play, emotion, and communication to children with autism.* Arlington, TX: Future Horizons.

Baker, J. (2006). *The social skills picture book for high school and beyond.* Arlington, TX: Future Horizons.

Bellini, S. (2006). *Building social relationships: A systematic approach to teaching social interaction skills to children and adolescents with autism spectrum disorders and other social difficulties.* Shawnee Mission, KS: AAPC Publishing.

Bellini, S., Peters, J. K., Benner, L., & Hoph, A. (2007). A meta-analysis of school-based social skills interventions for children with autism spectrum disorders. *Journal of Remedial and Special Education, 28,* 153-162.

Benton, M., Hollis, C., Mahler, K., & Womer, A. (2012). *Destination friendship: Developing social skills for individuals with autism spectrum disorders or other social challenges.* Shawnee Mission, KS: AAPC Publishing.

Brewer, R., & Mueller, T. (2008). *Strategies at hand: Quick and handy strategies for working with students on the autism spectrum.* Shawnee Mission, KS: AAPC Publishing.

Buron, K. (2007). A "5" could make me lose control! Shawnee Mission, KS: AAPC Publishing.

Buron, K. (2007). *A 5 is against the law.* Shawnee Mission, KS: AAPC Publishing.

Buron, K., & Curtis, M. (2009). *5-point scale and anxiety curve poster.* Shawnee Mission, KS: AAPC Publishing

Carter, M. A., & Santomauro, J. (2010). *Friendly facts: A fun, interactive resource to help children explore the complexities of friends and friendship.* Shawnee Mission, KS: AAPC Publishing.

Cattlet, S., Cheramie, G., Coleman, C., Mitchell, V., & Sheridan, S. J. (2008). *Autism IEP: Additional strategies for consideration.* Houston, TX: Region 4 Educational Service Center.

Charlop, M. H., & Trasowech, J. E. (1991). Increasing autistic children's daily spontaneous speech. *Journal of Applied Behavior Analysis, 24,* 747-761.

Clark, R. (2003). *The essential 55.* New York, NY: Hyperion.

Clark, R. (2004). *The excellent 11.* New York, NY: Hyperion.

Cohen, S. (2002). Social relationships and health. *American Psychologist, 54,* 676-684.

Constantino, J. N., & Gruber, C. P. (2005). *Social responsiveness scales (SRS).* Los Angeles, CA: Western Psychological Services.

Endow, J. (2010). *Practical solutions for stabilizing students with classic autism to be ready to learn: Getting to go!* Shawnee Mission, KS: AAPC Publishing.

Grandin, T., & Barron, S. (2005). *Unwritten rules of social relationships: Decoding social mysteries through the unique perspectives of autism.* Arlington, TX: Future Horizons.

Gray, C. (1994). *Comic strip conversations: Illustrated interactions that teach conversation skills to students with autism and related disorders.* Arlington, TX: Future Horizons.

Hart, B., & Risley, T. R. (1975). Incidental teaching of language in the preschool. *Journal of Applied Behavior Analysis, 8,* 411-420.

Hodgdon, L. (2008). *Visual strategies for improving communication.* Troy, MI: QuirkRoberts Publishing.

Jones, A. (1998). *104 activities that build: Self-esteem, teamwork, communication, anger management, self-discovery and coping skills.* Richland, WA: Rec Room Publishing.

Koegel, R. L., & Koegel, L. K. (2006). *Pivotal response treatments for autism. Communication, social, & academic development.* Baltimore, MD: Paul H. Brookes Publishing.

Kranowitz, C. (1995). *101 activities for kids in tight spaces.* New York, NY: Skylight Press.

Krantz, P. J., MacDuff, M. T., & McClannahan, L. E. (1993). Programming participation in family activities for children with autism: Parents' use of photographic activity schedules. *Journal of Applied Behavior Analysis, 26,* 137-138.

Mahler, K. (2009). *Hygiene and related behaviors for children and adolescents with autism spectrum and related disorders.* Shawnee Mission, KS: AAPC Publishing.

McClannahan, L. E., & Krantz, P. J. (2005). *Teaching conversation to children with autism.* Bethesda, MD: Woodbine House.

McConnell, S. R. (2002). Interventions to facilitate social interaction for young children with autism: Review of available research and recommendations for educational intervention and future research. *Journal of Autism and Developmental Disorders, 32,* 351-372.

Moyes, R. A. (2001). *Incorporating social goals in the classroom.* Philadelphia, PA: Jessica Kingsley Publishers Ltd.

Myles, B. S., & Simpson, R. (1993). Integrating preschool children with autism with their normally developing peers: Research findings and best practices recommendations. *Focus on Autistic Behavior, 8,* 1-19.

Notbohm, E. (2006). *Ten things your student with autism wishes you knew.* Arlington, TX: Future Horizons.

Quill, K. A. (2000). *Do-watch-listen-say: Social and communication intervention for children with autism.* Baltimore, MD: Paul Brookes Publishing Co.

Schopler, E., Mesibov, G. B., & Hearsey, K. (1995). Structured teaching in the TEACCH system. In E. Schopler & G. B. Mesibov (Eds.), *Learning and cognition in autism* (pp. 243-267). New York, NY: Kluwer Academic/Plenum.

Shafer, M. S., Egel, A. L., & Neef, N. A. (1984). Training mildly handicapped peers to facilitate changes in the social interaction skills of autistic children. *Journal of Applied Behavior Analysis, 17,* 461-476.

Simpson, R. L., de Boer-Ott, S. R., Griswold, D. E., Myles, B. S., Byrd, S. E., Ganz, J. E., Cook, K. T., Otten, K. L., Ben-Arieh, J., Kline, S. A., & Adams, L. G. (2005). *Autism spectrum disorders: Interventions and treatments for children and youth.* Thousand Oaks, CA: Corwin Press.

Texas Statewide Leadership for Autism. (2008). *Texas autism research guide for effective teaching (TARGET).* Retrieved from http://www.txautism.net

Vermeulen, P. (2012). *Autism as context blindness.* Shawnee Mission, KS: AAPC Publishing.

Volkmar, F. R., Paul, R., Klin, A., & Cohen, D. (2005). *Handbook of autism and pervasive developmental disorders* (3rd ed., Vols. 1 and 2). Hoboken, NJ: John Wiley and Sons Inc.

Wetherby, A. M., & Prizant, B. M. (2000). *Autism spectrum disorders: A transactional developmental perspective.* Baltimore, MD: Paul H. Brookes Publishing Co.

Wilkes, A. (2006). *Children's quick and easy cookbook.* New York, NY: DK Children.

Winner, M. G. (2000). *Inside out: What makes a person with social cognitive deficits tick?* San Jose, CA: Author.

Winner, M. G. (2002). *Thinking about you thinking about me: Teaching perspective taking and social thinking to persons with social cognitive learning challenges* (2nd ed.). San Jose, CA: Think Social Publishing.

Winner, M. G. (2009). *A politically incorrect look at evidence-based practices and teaching social skills: A literature review and discussion.* San Jose, CA: Think Social Publishing.

P.O. Box 23173
Shawnee Mission, Kansas 66283-0173
www.aapcpublishing.net